WHAT PEOPLE ARE S

What the Hell is Hell?

"I have never felt so compelled to leave a review for a book as I did for this one. It didn't so much change my life as renew, reinvigorate, reinspire, and reawaken me! Since childhood I've had a fear of not being good enough or solid enough in my faith to be sure I wouldn't go to hell when I die. This book showed me directly from scripture that much of what I had been taught did not come from Jesus, but was fabricated later by people misunderstanding so much of what he said.

"One thing I can tell you for sure: There will be many most unexpected moments when you will know deeply in your heart and soul that God is indeed speaking to you through these words. It has been and continues to be an ongoing blessing in my life, as well as for my husband and family."

Andrea Dacey, RD,CSSD, Sports Dietitian
Boston, MA

"The love that pours forth in these pages is both profound and illuminating. *What the Hell is Hell?* shows us that the doctrines of fear put forth by many religious leaders are not the actual intent or content of Jesus's words. This book empowers readers to know God personally. If you find any parts challenging, stick with it—the gifts of this book could change your life."

Lisa Tener, Award Winning Author
Saunderstown, R.I.

"You made me tear up many times. Your book stirred up so much good feeling that I don't have words for…this is amazing.

I have never so understood the words 'seek and you shall find' as I do now. You made me appreciate my life in the present, rather than fear what will happen when I die. Your message is beautiful. Thank you."

Juan Velasco, *Carlsbad, CA*

"This book is a beautiful dive into spirituality and a great introduction to embracing love and letting go of fear, ego, and misconceptions. Thought provoking and very well written, you will not be disappointed!"

Atalie Friedrich, *Escondido, CA*

"As a person who grew up a believer of the Christian faith, I was always afraid to express or discuss many of the questions I had carried for a lifetime. I'm all in for taking a leap of faith, but many teachings just didn't seem right. Church, Bible study, self-study didn't help. I felt half in and half out of my spiritual self. Finally, I was led to *What the Hell is Hell?* I cried and laughed as I revisited my childhood fears as an adult. I love the messages in this book! When I got to the end, I felt whole, loved, and complete. I now feel excited and confident in my faith."

Debby Parks, *Westerville, OH*

"If you enter this book with an open mind, you will be forced to reexamine your ideas about salvation and your true relationship with God. We were not put on this earth to blindly accept centuries' old religious dogma, but to use our God-given mind to study and search how to truly know and interact with God. When you finish *What the Hell is Hell?* you will be inspired to study the Gospels from a refreshed and inspired perspective."

Greg Kritzer, *San Diego, CA*

What the Hell is Hell?

A Non-Religious Look at the Facts,
and the Love that Shows
You How to Soar

Kevin Grant

Paperback ISBN: 9781737082040
Library of Congress Control Number: 2024901373

All the scripture quotations contained herein are from these two Bibles:

Quotes from either Bible are used interchangeably throughout this book. The choice of which to use was often based on which seemed easier to understand.

I invite you to take a fresh look at Jesus' words, his loving messages, and to be reminded of God's plain truth that there is no place for fear in love.

CONTENTS

PREFACE FOR THE NEW EDITION

Have you loved God your whole life but also had a lurking fear of hell? Do you believe that if you don't hold just the right beliefs, or if you're not a good enough person, you could roast in fire for all eternity? That is terrifying, and it's why this book came to be.

If you have such fear to any degree, *What the Hell is Hell?* can take it away from you forever, simply by showing you what Jesus actually said about hell. But even if hell is something you only wonder about from time to time, its meaning in the Bible will be made perfectly clear. And you'll see that a touch of levity and much love is called for here, because most of what's been feared about hell, going back nearly two millenia, is not supported by the Bible. This subject, however, being important enough on its own, is also just the gateway to a remarkable journey you will take through these pages, in a unique experience.

When you are halfway through reading this book, we will have covered, with relative ease, all the essential scripture that contributes to your knowing for certain what Jesus said, and did not say, about hell. To know what he said, we have to know what he meant, and both the Old and New Testaments can shed much more light on that than is generally known. And yet, this text was born out of purely spiritual messages that you will also read, which came long before my years of intensive Bible study that would later confirm their truth.

I said this book *can* take your fear away, and not *will* take it away, because it is going to be up to you to receive the information that will take away the fear—to allow yourself to accept what you find. I will tell you up front: this book is never going to claim there is no hell. What it *is* going to do is show you that what Jesus spoke about, which was translated into our English Bibles as "hell," is not what most people who believe in hell believe it to be—namely, a place where one could burn in fire for all eternity after they die.

Once you know the truth of what Jesus was saying on this matter, it will set you free from any fear or belief you may have had about the possibility of an afterlife in such a place, which can only deepen your love and connection with God. It will also give you refreshed eyes and clarity as together we explore more of his teachings, many of which may take on new life for you. You'll be reawakened to the truth of your own unlimited spiritual potential, and you will know this is what Jesus taught, based on your own firsthand experience.

It might seem as if I just described a religious experience offered to you here but, ironically, there is no religious context intended for any of the material in this book. That is not a knock on religion in any way; it's just that this is about you.

More than just receiving information here, you will process spiritual truth for yourself, which won't require any specific belief system, nor should it interfere with your belief in Jesus, God, or whatever your faith may be.

I recognize that some of what's been said so far, as well as what's to come, may conflict with your beliefs or cause discomfort. If so, I can only ask you for a bit of trust in advance that I do not take your (or anyone's) sacred beliefs lightly. Please know also that I am not one to pick and choose verses of scripture and arrange them to conveniently make the Bible say what I'd like it to. Nor do I carelessly play upon your fear of hell and fabricate easy answers to comfort you. There is no conclusion about hell in this book that is not well supported by the Bible, and you will be able to verify the information for yourself.

Many people who read the first edition of *What the Hell is Hell?* have emailed me or posted reviews online saying they were helped by it—informed biblically or spiritually, or even that it changed their lives. Some said they were freed from a lifetime of fear, which was my deepest desire in writing it.

Those testimonials kept me going in my own most difficult moments of fear and doubt about the publishing of this book. It's been a harder road personally and professionally than I ever imagined it could be. My heartfelt thanks to all of you who took the time to share your thoughts and experiences with me.

I found God at a young age and felt his love and presence in my life. Yet I couldn't understand why our relationship with God always had to include this inherent fear of eternal damnation. Why would a loving God allow such incomprehensible torment to befall us if we were not able to live up to the standards he set for us or if we didn't know exactly what beliefs to hold?

There came a day when God spoke to me about these and many other matters. Now, I realize how that sounds, believe me, but I don't know how else to say it here but plainly, and there will be much more explanation to come (including what I even mean by "God"). Although you'll be seeing those messages throughout this book, they have nothing to do with proving what Jesus said about hell. Yet, by seeing how much the messages have benefited others, I know they were not meant for me alone.

I'm as flawed as any human being, but I have always striven to seek and grow, and have done so with a healthy skepticism. Yet I believed in what I was experiencing when the messages first came. The information came so powerfully that somehow I knew it was true, but I didn't yet have the knowledge to corroborate it (biblically or spiritually). As a result, I eventually spent many thousands of hours doing research in order to see if the information I'd received was supported by the Bible and in harmony with what Jesus taught, coupled with my own personal seeking of a few decades.

If you have wrestled with the same confusion over how a God who loves us could punish us so horrifically and mercilessly, and you would like some answers, you will receive them—right here, right now.

When you read the evidence in the Gospels for yourself, you will see that much of what we fear the most was our own creation. It's hard for us to accept that God's love is as the sun, and our fear is like tissue paper we try to drape upon it.

You will know that Jesus' paramount purpose—besides teaching us to love others—was ever guiding us to live our best lives, to find our own answers, and fulfill our own personal spiritual growth. That is what he meant when he told us to love God. It was not a religious message but a universal message of eternal wisdom, standing high and above any specific theology. For to love God is to love ourselves, which is to learn, grow, and trust in God, and which can be called a road to salvation.

This book speaks to those who believe in God and are versed in the New Testament; however, if you are someone who has lost your faith in God (whatever particular faith it was), or if you have never believed in God, or even if you simply have a secular interest in the teachings of Jesus, I encourage you to read this book with no preconceptions about what it will tell you. There is nothing in it that proclaims you ought to believe in Jesus or God.

Let us all, for the moment, not allow others, or even the whole of religious history, to tell us what Jesus meant. Instead, let's agree to look at his words as if for the first time.

I also want to add here that, when we have a new book in our hands, we are sometimes tempted to peek ahead or flip to the end to see where the book is going. In this case, I highly recommend that you refrain from doing so. The people who wrote in with the most extraordinary experiences with *What the Hell is Hell?* had stayed the course, and said in various ways that there was a magic of syncronicity that happened with the natural progression of the text and the revelations they had as it unfolded. Reading the messages out of order could rob you of the best this book has to offer.

I hope you, too, will have a transformative experience. But, at the very least, if you presently live in fear of the possibility of burning in hell for eternity after you die, may you be clear on what Jesus had to say about that.

Love is the only way to truly understand the Gospel of Jesus, and if you are not sure of that now, I hope you will be when you finish this book.

With love,
Kevin Grant
October 27, 2024

INTRODUCTION

My path with Christianity began when I was seven years old. I did not grow up in a religious home; we were Jewish by heritage, but no one in my immediate family believed in God. I did, however, have a very loving babysitter, who happened to be Christian. My parents had been freshly divorced, which left my siblings and me unsupervised a lot, and I had an older brother who used to beat me up almost daily. One Sunday, my babysitter knew that when she left I was going to be neglected and an open target, and she somehow arranged to take me back to her house for the day. When we arrived, her relatives and lots of friends were there. It turned out that it was Easter (I didn't know at the time what Easter was). These events led to one of the most powerful and vivid memories of my life.

After being at her home for a while, I wandered out onto her driveway and, standing there alone, I perceived a distinct, tangible feeling in the air that was totally new and fascinating to me. I was too young to have the words for it, but I knew it was love, and yet more than that; it felt as if I were standing on some ethereal plain in another dimension, extending endlessly in every direction around me. In retrospect, I know it was my first contact with Spirit, which I would go on to spend much of my life seeking to understand.

Somewhere in my teens, my need for understanding led to an insatiable thirst for knowledge about Jesus. I started reading the Bible, watched various preachers on TV, and had as many conversations as I could with adult Christians. I became enthralled with the teachings and story of Jesus. His words resonated profoundly with me—there was something special and captivating about them—and by the time I was about seventeen years old, his lead and his teachings became main staples on my spiritual path.

In my early twenties, I tried several churches of different denominations. It was interesting and beneficial to experience the various ways services were conducted and to listen to different kinds of sermons. I eventually found a church I liked, which I attended with some regularity (not every Sunday). At some point, however, I began to sense contradictions between my own spiritual experience and what was being said in many of the sermons I heard.

From the time I began down this path, I accepted the divinity of Jesus, and also that he was a man, as it said in the Bible. His words, which were printed red in our Bibles, seemed to shine with truth and goodness. Yet, in most of his Sunday sermons, our preacher would make it clear that unless I accepted Jesus Christ as my Savior, I would not make it into heaven, which meant I would burn in hell for all eternity.

Something about that didn't seem right to me. How did those four long books called the Gospels (Matthew, Mark, Luke, John), which contain all the words of Jesus we have, get reduced to this one terrifying ultimatum? Among all the words written in red ink, there were only a few that mentioned this threat of a fiery damnation. And when Jesus did speak of that judgment, it was to come at the end of the world as we know it. Primarily, though, he seemed focused on love and spiritual development.

In addition to the threat of damnation, we were usually reminded that Jesus Christ was the only way to God. But since we were all at church already, I didn't understand why we needed to be constantly remind of that. Was the main purpose of church simply to teach and keep us aware that this was the only way to God and heaven?

Jesus said, "Ask and it will be given to you; seek and you will find; knock and the door will be opened to you."[1] Eventually I decided to put those words into practice and ask God for the answers to my questions. I also studied the Bible incessantly and researched its history and the meaning of its words.

It took many years of seeking and learning before I received a whole slew of answers in a most unexpected way. At the time, I lived on the coast of New Hampshire and had a business importing and exporting seafood. I had driven up to Canada to visit a supplier. As I drove home, about five hours had passed of the nine-hour ride. I had been listening to the radio, perhaps daydreaming about religious questions, when a forceful voice in my head said, *Stop the music.*

I grabbed a notebook I had with me and, as though I were recording someone talking, I held the wheel with one hand while using the other to write down messages that were coming through. They were teachings that directly answered the questions and concerns I had about my beliefs. When I

1 Matthew 7:7; Luke 11:9.

realized this wasn't stopping any time soon, I pulled off the road to a rest area. The information was coming at such a speed that I could barely get it down on paper fast enough. I knew the words were not my own because I did not know any of the information being provided. I remember thinking, *Where is this coming from?*

I believe a great many of us are tired of hearing people claim to have received communications from a source higher than themselves. We've all had more than our share of crazy, harmful self-righteousness in this world. But we also can't let the fanatics silence the wisdom to be gained from seekers. I believe the words I received came from God. Perhaps they came only because I was at a place on my path to be ready to receive them, and they were the genesis of this book. But it is not for me to tell you to believe they are God's words, nor is it actually too relevant as to what they mean. The words themselves are all that matter, and you can determine both their value to you and where they came from.

The messages I wrote down were like gusts of fresh air and common sense, which put to rest most of the inner conflicts that had plagued me about what I ought to believe. Later, the words scared me, because I believed I might be risking the fate of my soul just by listening to them. What I was being told went against some of the fundamental beliefs that for many years I'd been taught God commanded for me to hold.

When I got home that night, I put my notebook away in a closet, where it remained for nearly a decade. Periodically the words I'd written down called out to me, but every time I started to type them up, the same fears would arise. State publicly that I received messages from God, or even from

Spirit? No thanks. Besides that, the fundamental beliefs and doctrines those messages threw into question traced back almost two thousand years, and I had to ask myself, *Who do you think you are to address such things?*

Fortunately, my relationship with God did not begin or end with that one experience in the car. I know God has always been with me, and was with me throughout the writing of this book. Many times when I was stuck for hours or days trying to express a spiritual point, I would pray for clarity and it actually came.

⚘⚘⚘⚘⚘⚘

What the Hell is Hell? is written for anyone who can gain value from it. There is no greater ambition here than for you to benefit by reading it. I don't presume to know who you are or what your experience has been. When I started to write this book, I struggled for countless hours to convey the material in a way that would speak to all people regardless of their religious background or beliefs and would not offend anyone. In short, I was trying to play it safe, but no matter how hard I tried, the messages would then lose potency in my religiously correct translation. That struggle ended when I realized I didn't have to be concerned about anyone else's beliefs—only my own. All I had to do was stay true to the material as it resonated with me.

Your beliefs might be different from mine, or perhaps you have no beliefs about God or Jesus, but for our purposes in this book that doesn't matter. While I speak to you mostly in

Christian terminology, the themes and messages presented here are universal. I don't speak from or address any particular denomination, because doing so might elicit preconceptions—it might let religion get in our way. And although this book searches for truth in the context of Christianity, it is not a religious book.

It is certainly, however, a spiritual book.

The voice I heard in my head that day spoke as God, as a guide, as a friend, and as Spirit itself, all of which I have come to find are one and the same. Sometimes the voice was loving and gentle, sometimes funny, and sometimes powerfully serious in speaking to what has been and continues to be taught and done in God's name.

Religious fanaticism and denial of reason or intellect have always bothered me, yet I believe in God with all I am. Those who know God a bit find no contradiction here (those who don't believe in God find nothing but contradiction here). As an avid seeker, I've learned plenty from books, teachers, scholars, lyrics, movies, plays—the taxi driver I spoke to last night—all kinds of people and sources. It just so happens that the majority of my spiritual growth has come through the words attributed to Jesus in the Bible. I revere him greatly, dearly, and profoundly. I can't help loving him. As I strove to understand his words, I was transformed by their meaning. I find, however, those same words are misappropriated and used to divide people more than any other words I know.

Whether or not this book you are about to read contains the truth is for you to decide. If you were raised in or hold beliefs similar to those that have been mentioned here, and if you feel a tension between what you've been taught and your own thoughts and feelings about God, I hope these words will speak to you, and help you, as I have been helped.

Kevin Grant
February 9, 2019

As it is written, let us consider the lilies.

Can you know what a lily smells like if you have never smelled one? What if, from the time you were a small child, and throughout your life, without ever letting you smell one, I kept on describing to you what a lily smells like? What if I taught you all about its biological properties and how it grows from a seed to a flower? What if I taught you the mechanics of how fragrance arouses our sense of smell? What if I took you to greenhouses and let you smell hundreds of other flowers? Would you then know what a lily smells like? Imagine then you had to describe what a lily smells like.

For so many of us, that is not unlike what's been expected of us concerning our understanding of God. We grew up having to believe everything we were told about God before learning for ourselves whether it was true. This is faith, we were told. We've had to be able to state what we believe without hesitation. Yet, we can never know God by being told who God is, any more than we can know what a lily smells like without having smelled one ourselves.

That might seem like an amusing comparison, but God is deemed no laughing matter.

We were given reason to fear, and the reason still causes fear to this day. What could make us accept without question all we were taught about God were it not for a major threat being held over us? In this case the threat is beyond lethal—an eternity spent in hell rather than in heaven. The goodness of eternity in heaven might be reason enough to believe without question, but what's to become of us if we don't get into heaven? That is something to fear. And we were given heaven and hell as the only two options for what happens to us when we die.

We were told that only Jesus knew what a lily smelled like. But if we believed in him, and accepted all his words and all we were told about him, we would surely get to smell a lily too—in heaven. We were told how wonderful life would be—after we are dead.

Jesus himself, however, presented us with much better news: The lily is within reach for us to smell right now.

PART I

CHAPTER 1

THE BEGINNING OF THE PATH

Writing down those teachings in the car that day, it was as if I had unexpectedly come upon a house deep in the woods. It proved impossible for me to simply take you there as a reader on page one; I first had to clear a path to it by providing context for understanding the information there. For some, that path will be old, familiar territory; for others it will be a new route. There are, however, some teachings interspersed along the way where they were called for. They are quoted exactly as I recorded them in my notebook and are set apart from the main text in this different font.

As you begin reading *What the Hell is Hell?*, I hope you are relaxed, at peace, and that we can even have a little fun along the way.

You are alone right now in your head. Whether you are nestled in the comfort of your couch or sitting on a crowded train, no one can read your thoughts. There is no one to judge you for thinking about new ideas or rethinking old ones. There is no one to interfere with your experience here. You are free.

> Please know I am a God of love, not fear.
> Please don't believe there are any thoughts
> you could think that could condemn your soul.
> Please don't confuse discussing, questioning,
> or examining your religious beliefs with having
> a lack of faith.

Let's say you want to be able to drive a car. You take a driver education course, you watch instructional videos, and you listen to lectures on driving. Will that make you a good driver? No. It's all of no value until the knowledge can be applied. You can never be a good driver without the *experience* of driving.

Likewise, you can read the Bible cover to cover, read all the books written on the subject of spirituality, listen to every sermon and lecture, but you can only gain spiritual knowledge when you have experienced spirituality for yourself.

"Seek and you will find."

Why are these words in the Bible? Why are they so powerful that they are among the most quoted words over the many centuries since Jesus lived? Throughout the Gospels, he guides you to seek God; he wants you to find answers for yourself; he wants you to come to know God through your own experience of God, as I hope you'll see and know in your heart by the end of this book, if you don't know already.

What you've been told about God all your life may be correct. Whoever told you probably had good intentions. The question is, do you know that what you've been told is correct? Or have you simply reconciled yourself to believing it is, because faith is all that matters?

Either way, everything you've been told about God can help to prepare you—to inspire you—to find God for yourself, if you so desire. This is not to say that any one of us is going to find a being called God appearing before us. It's more like saying we can come to perceive God, and find spiritual truth to which we can relate, and wisdom we can incorporate into our lives, as we grow more aware of who we are.

There are almost no easy answers to questions about God. I believe "God is Love" is one of the few that are easy, but how can that be proven? And even if we could prove it, it wouldn't mean we fully understand who or what God is. We cannot know God completely, yet, slowly, over time, we can develop a deepening relationship with God, which is to say, a Spirit that is always teaching us, or a Source we can endlessly learn from.

In your search for spiritual understanding as pertains to your own life, there is no question you can ask God that God will not answer: Which are God's words? What do any particular words in the Bible mean? Who is Jesus? What does righteous mean?

The more you ask, the more answers you'll receive. You control your progress—the distance you travel on your path as

WHAT THE HELL IS HELL?

a seeker, and the speed with which you traverse it, are up to you. You can spend an hour a day seeking, or you can spend a collective hour over the whole of your life. The more you seek, the more you will find. Walking this path is your spiritual life.

⸙⸙⸙⸙⸙⸙⸙

For much that you are taught in life, you test it through trial and error, see immediate results, and learn. If you were taught as a child not to touch a pot on a hot stove, but you did it anyway, you got burned and learned a lesson. If someone gives you correct driving directions, except for the last turn that was a right instead of a left, you find out quickly you were accidentally led astray.

Unfortunately, though, when it comes to spiritual matters, it seems you will have to wait until you are dead to find out if anything you've been taught is incorrect, and by then it will be too late to go back and correct those mistakes.

If you had believed in a heaven belonging only to those who accepted Jesus Christ as their Savior, and you were right, you'll be spending eternity in a private Eden with your fellow believers while everyone else goes to hell. Any of your friends, family, and all other souls who didn't believe in Jesus will be burning and wailing in torment, but there will be nothing you, as a citizen of heaven, can do about it. Someone might put his arm around you and say, "No need to let the suffering of the unfaithful dampen the mood in Paradise."

Or, what if your belief in the divinity of Jesus Christ was spot on, but the seeking Jesus preached about was also important and you didn't do much of it? More than weeping and gnashing your teeth at the gates of heaven, you might want to smack your forehead in frustration.

Spiritual growth depends on accepting one simple truth: we cannot know what we do not yet know. We can pretend to know. We can believe, talk, and act as if we know. In the end, however, if we don't know, we will just have been fooling ourselves. If we want answers, the first step is to be aware we don't have them—to be honest about having questions.

I had been taught that if you believed in Jesus you would be saved. No seeking was required, because all spiritual knowledge had already been delivered, and every spiritual question had been answered long ago.

That kind of thinking, however, made less sense the more I accepted the truth: I had no personal knowledge that the answers I'd been given were true. And I wanted to know—badly. I had to believe if anyone had ever found those answers, I could find them as well. I decided to be honest and get clear on what I knew and didn't know. For example, I knew the Bible said that Jesus gave a few blind men sight. I didn't know for sure if it really happened. I knew the Bible said that Jesus was God's Son. While I could believe this, I didn't know for myself whether it was true, or what it actually meant. The more I traced my beliefs to their roots, the more I realized that much of what I believed was what I had been taught to believe. When it came down to what I knew for myself to be true, I found I knew very little, and the more I did find, the more I realized there is always infinitely more to learn.

Assuming there is new knowledge to be gained, how can you receive it if your mind is closed? If you're sure you have all the answers already, how can there be anything left to learn? There is a new commandment to adopt if your purpose is spiritual development: Thou shalt have an open mind.

If you are truly growing, it means you are constantly new. Think of a tree that is constantly growing new branches, which leaf each season. With each new branch the tree is different from what it was before. Yet all the growth of the past (whatever you learn, right or wrong, or whatever your circumstances have been) has become a solid and unchanging foundation. The growth is a new extension of an old familiar tree. Based on that growth you can correct mistakes, learn from your past, or process new information. Like the tree, as you grow you retain the comforting stability of the self that still is and has always been. You do not lose yourself just because you acquire new information and allow for new growth.

Nevertheless, having an open mind can create conflicts with the religious beliefs we were raised in. I once had a colleague I will call Pat who was a devout man, and we became friendly. Over the course of a few lunches together, I learned that he had a strong-willed, religious mother, and, at forty-two, his beliefs about God were exactly what he'd been taught growing up, which were then reinforced at church ever since.

He had told me several times in our conversations that holding beliefs and thinking were not to be confused—there were some things that weren't our place to think about in a questioning manner.

One day I asked him, "What if you were taught that to grow spiritually you must have an open mind?"

Pat glared at me with self-righteousness and said, "Tell that to God."

As a result of what he'd been taught, Pat believed that God commands only one way to salvation and to even entertain the idea of having an open mind is to defy him.

Ironically, however, not having an open mind is what defies and denies God. The only thing most of us know about God is what our religion has told us; only by being open can we be ready to receive what *God* has to tell us. To be a traveler on the path towards knowing God personally, we must surrender all pretense of knowing what we do not know.

That is to say:

You can never know what lies ahead of you,
You are walking down a path you have never been
   down before,
You will come to know the path only after you have
   walked it.

It takes a brave heart to walk the path of spiritual seeking. Besides the fact that you will be moving into uncharted territory for yourself, you may have to confront a lifetime of being indoctrinated into a particular belief system and the threat of dire consequences that may result from questioning what you've been taught.

The words Jesus speaks in the Gospels, "Seek and you will find," are derived from the Old Testament: "From there you will seek the Lord your God, and you will find him if you search after him with all your heart and soul."[1] This seems to say that you should search for God and understanding, and perhaps that means both inside and outside of scripture, as well as through your own thoughts.

Yet I had been taught the same thing Pat was taught: Narrow is the way (God commands only one way to salvation) and being open to sources of information outside of what we were taught is to travel a wide path to damnation. While Jesus taught us to seek God, we were already told what we would find—as if all the work had already been done for us. The narrow path we were taught tended to be not a path of spiritual growth but of submission to and blind acceptance of a specific set of beliefs, which, we were told, would get us into heaven.

The idea of the narrow way comes from when Jesus tells us to "Enter through the narrow gate; for the gate is wide and the road is easy that leads to destruction, and there are many who take it. For the gate is narrow and the road is hard that leads to life, and there are few who find it."[2]

The spiritual truth of the narrow path has gone awry. "Narrow" refers to the individuality of your own path—a path you walk alone, with discipline and perseverance, doing the right things to take care of yourself, and staying true to the knowledge you have gained through experience. There is only one way for *you* to go in order to arrive at your own relationship with Spirit. There is wisdom and direction that can apply

---

1 Deuteronomy 4:29.
2 Matthew 7:13–14.

to all, but you need to find the way forward for yourself. That said, if you believe in God, you know you are not alone in your journey.

⌁⌁⌁⌁⌁⌁⌁

Seeking and keeping an open mind does not preclude us from using the Bible as our primary source of spiritual knowledge. After all, we are talking about what Jesus meant when he was instructing us to seek, and the Bible contains all the words of his that we have. He said, "the pure in heart will see God."[3] What could be purer than coming to God with an open and humble mind and asking him for the answers, even if we've already been given the answers by others?

Also, walking our own path does not conflict with going to church. There is a sense of community in church, of being with like-minded neighbors, a congregation with whom to feel love, and a preacher who can teach God's words. Those can all serve our well-being as we find our way forward. And yet, at the same time, God is available to us anywhere, and requires nothing more than our being open and desirous to find understanding.

Jesus preached, "When you pray, go into your room, close the door and pray to your Father, who is unseen."[4] By doing this, you are in intimate communication with God. He said, "When you are praying, do not heap up empty phrases as the Gentiles do; for they think that they will be heard because of

---

3 Matthew 5:8.
4 Matthew 6:6.

their many words."[1] In other words, do not pray in a disingenuous by-the-numbers way, but rather in a genuine way. "Seek and you will *find*." In these examples you can see his intention for you to develop a personal relationship with God.

Another benefit of keeping an open mind is a wealth of resources will be available to you. You can tap into every bit of information you receive about God, extract what you find to be valuable, and leave the rest behind. You can study the works of all the great thinkers from all the ages on the subjects of religion, spirituality, and philosophy. How better to substantiate what to believe and why, than to gather as much knowledge as you can, and from different points of view?

If, on the other hand, your mind is closed, you will only ever be validating what you've already been told to believe. It's as if someone said to you, "Tell me if this painting is the finest painting in the museum, but you can't look at any of the other paintings. And by the way, if you don't say it's the finest painting, you will burn in hell."

It is a sad and oppressive teaching that having an open mind can cost you your salvation. You may have questions such as "Is God real?" "How did we get here?" "Was Jesus the Messiah?" Despite being given the answers to these questions by the Bible, how could it be considered a lack of faith to verify them for yourself—through your own inner searching, prayer, or through outside sources? Surely God would welcome any means necessary to help you understand that his answers are true.

If you do not examine all the truths you are told about God, your soul, and how to live your life, how will you ever

---

1 Matthew 6:7.

learn for yourself whether the reasoning used to arrive at those truths is sound? Reason and spirituality are not mutually exclusive.

Are not truth, reason, and logic all part of God's creation? All part of God? Why would this supreme Creator imbue our universe with governing forces such as gravity and electromagnetism, occurring in such constancy that precise languages of mathematics and physics allow us to evolve technologically to benefit our lives, or to land a roving probe on Mars, but then, when it comes to contemplating Him, require us to stop using our minds?

God does not ask any of us to play dumb.

We must think about what we've been taught about God. Our thinking and reasoning are as necessary for understanding spiritual matters as they are for learning how to use a computer. God, and our relationship with God, are supposed to make sense. If we don't make that sense for ourself, we will have to settle for what we are told is the truth.

Your beliefs are yours; they are the foundation of who you are. *What the Hell is Hell?* is not meant to tell you what you should believe. It will give you the biblical documentation to see what Jesus actually said about hell, and other vital matters, which you can then verify for yourself. As for the messages you will read that are not from the Bible, you will have to trust your own intuition.

All I ask is for you to be open, be honest, and be yourself.

Allow yourself to stay in touch with your feelings without worrying about judgment. If something you read feels right and the documentation is sound, but it conflicts with what you believe or have been taught, at least follow the truth where it goes without fear—check up on it. If you believe God loves you unconditionally, you certainly have nothing to fear in reading or thinking about *any* words on your path to seeking the truth.

There may be much in this book you will agree with, but the time to really pay close attention is when you disagree or feel uncomfortable about something you read. Stop and explore the reasons for your feelings. If you are at peace with your beliefs, mere words shouldn't rattle you. If you are bothered, it might be that there is some aspect of your beliefs you have not thought through. As a result, you might take the time to do that and become stronger in your beliefs, knowing why you believe what you believe. In this way, even if the words you have read are wrong, they will have served you.

I have no stake in addressing the spiritual validity of any belief system, but at some point in our lives shouldn't each of us figure out and decide for ourselves what to believe? The only value of blind faith is to get us started. No one is rewarded for willingly abandoning reason and accepting what they are told without question. Such faith can render our spiritual life to be like a flower cut from its roots. It may look beautiful but has no life force to nurture it to grow in knowing God better.

For a long time I believed in God but questioned whether that belief was right. I didn't know for sure that God existed—at least in the way I was conceiving him. Sometimes "God" felt like the right word. Sometimes a great "Spirit" felt more accurate. The spiritual lessons I learned as a seeker were different from those I had heard preached. I still cannot fully comprehend God or Spirit, and will always be a seeker. Yet, based on my spiritual life and experience, I can now say with certainty that there is something more going on within this life than mere circumstance or reality, and within that something there is an organizing principle, love, benevolence, and guidance. I tend to refer to that something as either "God" or "Spirit" interchangeably.

I could write a personal treatise on all the astounding times Spirit has poked its way into my life—all the education I have received. I could write about spiritual perception or the internal experience of seeking and the rewards I have gained. But I don't think it's useful to delve into what could be viewed as subjective conjectures.

I can say that I simply cannot look at the world around me and take it all for granted—living on the coastline has made this especially true. Standing at the ocean's edge at sunset, gazing out at the mass of water rolling into shore, waves curl toward collapse as rainbows fly intermittently off their back-spray; the sinking giant sun aglow—performs its show, changing yellow, orange, red—streaking the sky in resplendent hues of pinks and purples, as pelicans soar along the coast in precision formation; the appreciation of my life and creation, and my utter inability to comprehend it all, leaves me in tears and shivering in awe. This is not poetry or purple prose; it's reality.

I don't then take that incomprehension and slap the name "God" on it for an answer, but for lack of a better word, "God" acknowledges there is more to creation than the reality we can observe or explain. Science can do a lot to explain the processes that govern our world and even how it came to be, along with the evolution of its lifeforms (including us), but it can't explain how those processes originated. No one can state with certainty how we (life) came to exist, we can only theorize. We can only hold beliefs about such matters. No one knows all the answers. No one. Yet to say there is nothing more to the spark of creation and its laws than mere chance is to ignore the fundamental mystery at the heart of it all, which can easily allow us to take it for granted. Would it be safe all around to say that life itself is a wonder beyond comprehension?

Sometimes using the word "God" can be problematic. God, even among believers, can be difficult to define. Going forward, however, I am going to be using the word God. At least for now, I ask you to refrain from jumping to conclusions about what that word means in this book. We are all constrained by the limits of our vocabulary to convey what we mean when we talk about God.

How can we define what God means when we cannot comprehend who or what God is? And what pronoun do we use in reference—"He," "She," "It"—what works?

God is real, but what does that mean? None would argue that something like a rock—something physical and solid—is real, but what about someone's feelings—sadness or love, for example. Aren't they real? What about the unseen forces that govern our reality (like gravity or even the inner workings of the atoms that comprise matter), do we call them real? Are these godly forces? And if we are spirit (have a soul), then don't we have something in common with God? How do you say some*thing* spiritual exists? God exists in another dimension, yet some of that dimension occupies the same "space" as we do and everything we know to be real. Umf!

Semantics can be a battle fought on a minefield. Therefore, it seems that discussing the failure of vocabulary as it relates to spiritual matters is a fitting way to continue this conversation.

CHAPTER 2

TERMS AND USAGE

Have you ever noticed how flippantly people use the word
"God?" How many times a week do you hear, "Oh my God,"
or, "God damn…" or, "As God is my witness…" I can't think
of any other word we use so often without being aware of what
we're saying. Even using the word in its proper context as in,
"I pray to God every Sunday," doesn't mean there is a clear,
well thought-out meaning behind it.

Another expression we use often is "Jesus Christ" to express an ineffable emotion. Maybe you've narrowly missed a
collision on the highway, or someone has done something
stupid, or you watched an Olympic snowboarder on TV soar
forty feet high while doing a triple back flip. I had a teacher in
grade school who lightly slapped our hands for saying it and
scolded, "Don't use the Lord's name in vain."

Despite such knee-jerk remarks, however, how many people do you know who say they believe in God but won't talk
much about who this God actually is? If you ask, "What does

'God' mean to you?" you are asking someone to explain their beliefs. For many people this is not easy or comfortable, unless they are among others who share their beliefs. For some, God may be too holy a subject for casual discussion (although that can be due to the fear of committing some offense against God that is at the root of their reluctance).

The limitations of our vocabulary are especially apparent when it comes to discussing subjects of a spiritual nature, because the same words can mean different things to different people. For example, to many, the meaning of the word "spiritual" is a generic adjective that could refer to any number of traditional religions. Many would say spiritual means a relationship with Jesus Christ—one might call music from a church "spiritual music." Others, however, might think spiritual refers to new-age practices, while still others associate the word spiritual simply with faith in God. For me, now, spiritual means having a present and participatory experience with Spirit: my *active* relationship with what we call God.

In many houses of worship of different faiths, the qualities of God are not open to mortal examination. We are told to hold beliefs without thinking them through, because God's words are to be accepted even if they are not understood. The less we question those beliefs, and the more we accept what we're taught, the more religious we're considered to be. Many of us simply abide by the beliefs or rules of whatever religion we were raised in, and may even be offended if someone speaks in any way we find disrespectful to those beliefs.

I don't believe we need to slap each other's hands for "using the Lord's name in vain," but perhaps we ought to be more aware when we're using "God" or "Jesus" in a loose manner.

If we are not, we might be in danger of operating with the same lack of awareness that allows us to espouse beliefs we haven't thought through for ourselves.

The Word God

"God" is just a word. Can we humbly accept this truth? To whom or what that word refers to is another matter. Some say God is a name for the Supreme Being, or Creator of our world and us. Some say God is a word that refers to the consciousness of Spirit. Some say God is the Father of Jesus. Some say God is nonsense. Even people with the same general beliefs, such as God is the Father of Jesus, might not agree on the specifics of what that means or how they define God.

If we are to arrive at a way of talking about God, we first have to determine what we can agree on concerning God. How can we grow in understanding without first grounding ourselves in what we already know?

What do we know about God? It takes humility and honesty to answer that question. Sometimes it means admitting what we don't know. Those of us who believe in God may have different beliefs about who or what God is, but none of us understands God very well. At best, we have tiny smatterings of knowledge and varying degrees of whatever relationship to God our little minds can handle. This is all relative, of course. A spiritual master will certainly know God a lot better than the average person. Yet a master would probably be the first to tell you that they don't come close to fully comprehending God. We can fully comprehend God as soon as we can lasso infinity.

God is the name you have given me. Remember,
God is a word and don't confuse that with who I
am. Say the word God to yourself, then observe
what that means to you. You have a definition
based on all the data you have gathered about
God throughout your life. It's good to have a
word that lets you refer to me, but do not let the
finite bounds of a word mislead you from the
truth of my infinite nature. Once I am labeled a
being—even a supreme being—a definition is
created. This can then tempt you to think that
because you do not see me in front of you, I am
therefore somewhere else far away from you.

How often do you stop and think about who or what this
God is that you so naturally say you believe in? Do you think,
No one can understand God, so why bother trying?

In the Old Testament, Moses asks God his name and God
responds "I am who I am,"[1] a phrase that has served to keep
alive the mystery and incomprehensibility of God.

Today, some religious Jews will write G-d rather than spell
out the name of the deity, because it serves an ages'-old tradition that forbids the name used for God to be written anywhere
it could be destroyed (or erased), but it also maintains a level
of respect and reverence, which keeps the word from being
taken lightly or its meaning oversimplified.

If we are to evolve spiritually, we can't be afraid to admit

---

1 Exodus 3:14.

that God is just a word. We cannot allow the nature of the principals (God, Spirit, Christ, et al.) to be limited by our vocabulary, which in turn is limited by our present understanding of those principals. It doesn't make sense to attribute irreverence to any honest and open conversation about the nature of God when we don't completely understand who or what we are talking about in the first place.

The Path Forward

Maybe we can start to arrive at an understanding of what God is by first agreeing on what God is not. Can we agree that God is not an old man with a long, flowing, gray beard, sitting on a throne in heaven? I believe most of us can agree on this.

The Bible states that we were created in God's image. This, like much in the Bible, has been taken literally by many of our religions. Therefore, literalist believers wouldn't subscribe to the notion that God is Spirit with no form. God's image has always been defined by our attempts to conceptualize him. Would it be any less correct, then, to say we made God in our image? The question has been asked for ages, but never seems less important for us to ask.

It's hard to imagine that, if God created this planet, all life on it, and perhaps all the universe and beyond, he is actually confined to the form of a human being, or any corporeal being. If there is an afterlife, though, and if, in that afterlife, there is any interaction with God (or perhaps lesser-emissary-godly beings), it seems sensible that they would assume human form, since this is the form most familiar to us. Perhaps then, the literal image of the strong, old, Zeus-like God would be an accommodation on his part for what our limited minds are able to comprehend, making his image a human old man, after all.

Or maybe he just began that way a trillion years ago.

In the end, no one can be sure of the form of God. Can we admit that much? Ultimately, it is just another mystery.

What else can we agree God is not?

God is not a He, She, or It.

God is somehow all of these and none of these; God cannot be fully covered by any one of them or all of them. We are off the pronoun chart when we refer to God, which is yet another indicator of how inadequate our vocabulary is for describing God.

He

God has been accepted as the Supreme Patriarch, the Father Creator of Humanity and all life, Infinite Mind, and, in Christianity, the Father of Jesus. We have an easy time associating masculine attributes with this God: discipline, strength, and power. He has been deemed the Authority, Judge, Ruler—the Supreme Administrator of all life on earth and in heaven. He loves us completely but is strict—we must obey his laws, commands, and his every word. He forces us to learn lessons for ourselves, won't pick us up when we fall, is there to guide, teach, and illuminate the way but will never do for us what we must do for ourselves. He is Father to us, as we are fathers to our children.

She

God is boundless love: unconditionally loving, nurturing, maternal, helping us again and again, always forgiving, and never turning away from us. Sometimes God is the only one who can, and does, help us up when we fall. We can alienate every human being in our lives but never God. She is Mother to us, as we are mothers to our children.

The Supreme Matriarchal nature of God was addressed in Christianity as the Holy Mother—the mother of Jesus. The mother Mary is not just a historical religious figure, but an eternal feminine spiritual essence, with all the characteristics of the quintessential loving mother.

If both male and female come from God, then doesn't it make sense that God is both of these? We know masculine and feminine energies are not exclusive to the actual gender of a human being. We know feminine energy can be prevalent in a man, and masculine energy prevalent in a woman. For most of us, one is more dominant than the other, but both masculine and feminine energies are present in virtually everyone. This reflects our likeness to God.

It

Then there is a third aspect of God that has no gender at all. This has often been called "the universe." Some people say, "The universe brought these two together," or, "The universe has a way of working things out." In spiritual practice, it has been called an energy field, a force, or universal Spirit. In Christianity, it has been called the Holy Spirit.

I like to think of the Holy Spirit as God's medium—the substance of God, so to speak, which is present in our world. It is here for us to interact with and relate to God. It is somehow the collective of all our consciousnesses; it is the love that binds us together (even if we are still a long way off from collectively realizing that). We can perceive and feel it—especially when we are gathered together in large groups, which might be at a place of worship, a concert, or even a movie. We can call upon it for assistance in our daily or spiritual lives: How can I be happier, healthier, wiser, more balanced, successful; how can I foster better relationships with people; how can I have Spirit more present in my life or understand God and his words better?

Spirit also exists neutrally (it just *is*) in that it only responds to how it is acted upon by us; it is a force of godly nature. This force has its own physics (of a sort) and laws. You can put it to work in your life. Maybe you've noticed that depending on where you direct your energy you receive dividends in that area. For example, you put your heart, mind, and drive into starting a new business or project, and somehow the right people seem to cross your path. Or, when you've declared the intention to seek knowledge in any area, the right book ends up in your hands at just the right time. Or, you've been injured and the doctor has told you it would take months to heal, or maybe that you'd never be the same, but by sheer determination you manage to defy that diagnosis.

There is much more to the truth of God than the being described and defined by monotheistic traditions. All over the world are examples of various spiritual forces at play, and people who have accessed the power of It. Thousands of people (myself included) have walked across red-hot burning embers with no harm. You can watch online videos of parades where multiple participants have long rods pierced through their cheeks with no blood coming out. You can watch documentaries about people who lie on a bed of nails without injury (even while a heavy man sits on their chest!), or others who hold their breath for inhuman amounts of time, or who endure other mind-boggling feats of physicality or endurance. I have twice in my life spoken to psychics who were complete strangers but knew intimate details about me and my thoughts they had no way of knowing, and made predictions that came precisely true years later (and I met a few others who were frauds).

He, She, and It are all aspects of the nature of God. Yet God is more than all of these. Who knows what other aspects of God lie beyond our comprehension? We cannot know what we don't know and are limited by our perception. Consider how we see a certain spectrum of light, yet we know there is more light that we don't see, such as infrared light. He, She, and It might be just three stars in the vast galaxy that is God.

The Impartiality of God's Love

Perhaps we can also state some basic characteristics of God that pertain to people. See if you agree with these:

GOD IS NOT ANY PARTICULAR RACE OR COLOR, OR PARTIAL TO ANY ONE OF THEM. God is every one of us and none of us, which makes sense if we are all God's children. How can you believe in God as Creator of all and then turn around and believe that any one particular group of people is less loved than another? God loves everyone equally.

GOD IS NOT PARTIAL TO ANY PARTICULAR BELIEF SYSTEM. No matter what names we want to call God, no matter how our beliefs differ, whether we believe nothing, or in something other than God—we are all the same human species. God loves us for who we are—not for what we believe.

GOD IS NOT PARTIAL TO ANY COUNTRY. Countries are simply different locations on the same earth, where the same one species of humans live. It is nonsensical to think that God would love any one country more than another.

GOD IS NOT PARTIAL TO MEN OR WOMEN. Although the Bible tends to favor men, sometimes to the point of misogyny, I believe we can finally be brave enough to put primitive ideas in their place and move on. God loves all people equally.

GOD DOES NOT PHYSICALLY INTERVENE IN THIS WORLD. Whether it's any ordinary person through meditation, the leader of a congregation, a monk, or a prophet, there have been and are many people who seek and indeed communicate with God, and who, based on those communications, learn and evolve, and sometimes proceed to enact change in the world. It also seems, at times, that God influences our thoughts even when we're not seeking. Whether or not we heed his words is another matter. So, in these ways, God does seem to influence the world. There also seems to be a providential design unfolding; sometimes events seem uncannily orchestrated. We experience inexplicable "coincidences" in our lives that guide and draw us toward God by way of curiosity and fascination.

Wouldn't you agree, however, that the hand of God does not reach down from the heavens and smite evildoers where they stand? Nor does God seem to physically protect innocent people from harm, or bring food, water, and medicine to suffering children. And history demonstrates that God will not prevent a genocidal lunatic from rising to lead a world power, or prevent any nation from committing genocide against another.

Let's review and see if we can agree on these aspects of what God is not:

- God is not an old man sitting on a throne in heaven.
- God is not a He, She, or It.
- God is not any one race or color, and is not partial to any.
- God is not partial to men or women.
- God is not partial to any particular country.
- God does not physically intervene in this world.

By contrast, let's see if we can agree on some characteristics of what God is:

- God is Love.
- God is with us always (guiding and inspiring us).
- God loves every person on earth equally:
  - God loves all races—every color, shape, and size.
  - God loves all nations.
  - God loves all people unconditionally regardless of what they believe (or do not believe).

God has additional qualities—dualities—that are a bit more complicated because they can seem contradictory, but I believe we can probably agree on them.

God is all good things: people loving one another, hugging, smiling, sharing, giving. God is light, happiness, warmth, the beauty of creation—the sunrise, sunset, oceans, rivers, forests, mountains, green lands, flowers, animals, aquatic life. God is the eternally benevolent Creator.

But if God created everything, God is also cold, darkness, misery, suffering, earthquakes, tsunamis, tornadoes, hurricanes, death. God is eternally indifferent.

God is the cutest Bambi deer balancing on his young new legs to sip from the pristine brook.

God is the lion ripping Bambi to pieces for food.

God is the beauty of all nature; God is the savagery of nature.

God designed our lives; God gave us free will.

God loves us; God allows terrible harm to come to us.

Do these few qualities of God seem basic enough that we can agree on them—at least to give us a common word we can work with? Anyhow, these are the qualities of the God I refer to in this book. Ultimately, however, God is beyond description. It is therefore important to remember that God is God, and we are only human. As humans, we would be wise to remember that "God" is just a word.

Jesus

Whether you believe he was God on earth or just a man, everyone can agree the name in the Bible refers to Jesus

Christ, which means Jesus the Messiah.[1] "Jesus," however, is also a name whose use it is easy to take for granted without examination.

The historical influence of Jesus is irrefutable. Leaving aside the issue of his divinity for a moment, the calendar governing most of the world was divided based on his birth (B.C. before Christ, and A.D. *anno Domini*, "in the year of the Lord"). For many of us, the grandest, most loving holiday of the year celebrates his birthday. Nearly a third of the planet's population believes him to be the most spiritually important figure who ever lived, and even non-Christians and those who don't believe in God would probably have to concede he was one of the most influential people in the history of Western culture, if not the most. Yet, the one we call Jesus never in his life on earth heard himself called by that name.

We have no way of being certain what Jesus' contemporaries called him, but we can make a strong educated guess because the name Jesus can be traced back to *Yeshua,* the Aramaic[2] form for the Hebrew name *Yehoshua.* The New Testament, however, was originally written in Greek. Therefore, *Yeshua* was transliterated into *Iesous.* In the first King James Bible published in 1611, we see Jesus' name as *Iesus* (the Latin version of the Greek *Iesous*). The letter J had not come into common use in English yet, but finally we first see the name "Jesus" in a later edition in 1629.

Put simply, Jesus is an English version of the Greek name *Iesous*, which is a Greek version of the Aramaic name *Yeshua.*

---

1 "Christ" is the English version of the Greek word *Christos,* which is a translation of the Hebrew word *Masiah,* meaning "annointed one."

2 The language Jesus and his people spoke.

Regardless of how we arrived at it, Jesus is the name we permanently settled on, and so, going forward, I will be using the name Jesus—the Son of God in the New Testament, the one who spoke the words that are printed in red in many of our Bibles.

What Is Truth?

Many of us were taught to accept as truth that Jesus spoke all the words attributed to him in the Bible and all the events of his life happened exactly as written. To do so was to have faith. "Did Jesus say this; did he say that?" "Did Pilate wash his hands?" "Did the Pharisees consider Jesus a threat?" "Did he walk on water?" "Did he raise the dead?" We were given the answers as they appear in the Bible. But having to accept those answers as truths left me confused. How could anyone call that which can never be verified for certain, the truth? As far as I could see, each of us was being asked to gloss over that problem by accepting the answers through faith.

According to many dictionaries:

truth: the quality or state of being true
(**true**: being in accordance with fact or reality)

Based on that definition, for any words attributed to Jesus in the Bible, such as, "Seek and you will find," it is the truth that those words are in the Bible. That Jesus actually said the words cannot be called the truth, because we have no way to know for certain, although we can say it's highly probable he said them. There is no attack on faith here. There is no denial of Jesus or God.

The truth is, we have words that were supposedly spoken by Jesus, written down decades after he died, and supposedly were passed down with precise accuracy through all the years in between. We must rely on those words having been perfectly translated from Aramaic into Greek, then later into English, even though these languages are fraught with semantic differences, nuances, and in many instances have no specific translation from one to the other, in order to arrive at a set of words we have no problem believing to be the absolute truth of what Jesus said and meant (the same problems hold true for any of the many other languages into which the original Greek was translated).

Many of us can easily accept this miracle—in defiance of the astronomical odds that this could have been accomplished without a single error—because, we say, God saw to it. God told the writers of the Gospels what Jesus said. God made sure everything was accurate. In fact, we say, God wrote the Bible.

We have to be brave enough to separate belief from truth. We can believe it is the truth that Jesus said what is attributed to him in the Bible. But what we believe to be the truth, of course, is not necessarily the truth. I believe it is the truth that Jesus said, "Ask and it will be given to you." But in truth not one of us knows for a fact that Jesus said any of those words. We can all believe that our faith has the ability to move mountains—juggle planets even—but we cannot invent truth. The truth is: We can believe that God wrote the Bible. The truth is: We can only believe. The truth is: We do not *know* God wrote the Bible.

I am not saying God did not write the Bible. I am not saying that Jesus did not speak all the words attributed to him in the Bible. I have never said whether or not I believe every single word in the Bible is the Word of God. All I did was to differentiate the concept of belief from truth, because it's easy to blur religious belief with historical fact and accept the Bible as absolute historical truth.

That said, when I speak about the words of Jesus, or the events of his life, I am not going to use words like *allegedly, supposedly, purportedly,* and so on. For example, "Jesus allegedly spoke the words _____." Although such caveats could well be applied to what was actually said and done two thousand years ago, when I refer to the words spoken by Jesus and the events of his life, please know I am referring to the words written in the Bible.

Also, it has been a nagging challenge for me to determine whether or not to capitalize the pronouns *he, him,* or *his* when writing about Jesus. While many people will think it slights the divinity of Jesus to not use the capital letter H every time, using it could be equally off-putting to those who don't believe in his divinity. The same challenge holds true for using the lowercase *him* as a pronoun for God. Even the simple matter of whether or not to use a capital letter can become a controversial issue of faith.

Using *he* to refer to God is also limiting God to a masculine understanding, which we've discussed in this chapter. What to do? I would use "he/she/it," as we have no better word, and at least it would keep us more aware of the ineffable nature of God, but that would get old and tedious fast, for both you and me, and so this pronoun issue is not a battle I choose to pick at this time.

To keep it simple, I use the lowercase letter h every time when referring to either God or Jesus as *he, him,* or *his.* Truthfully, I don't believe God would feel slighted if ever the usage was incorrect. I think he is above caring about our use of capitalization.

Spirit, Soul

There are a few terms used throughout this text whose meaning you probably intuitively know already. However, for the sake of clarity, I will briefly define these terms and how they'll be used in this book. In order to share an under-standing of the words "spirit" and "soul," we first have to have that working agreement on what "God" means. If you don't believe in God, the words spirit and soul might well be mean-ingless to you.

"Spirit" (capital S) will be used as a synonym for Holy Spirit. While occasionally the term Holy Spirit will be used, I usually prefer Spirit, because the word "Holy" can sometimes make it seem like something sacred to the point of being be-yond us, rather than something that is tangible and here for us to interact with. The word "spiritual" will mean of or per-taining to Spirit.

One's "spirit" (lowercase s) will mean an individuation of that Spirit—an individual life force inside a body. To refer to this individual spirit, I often use the word "soul." Whenever I refer to understanding something from the "level of soul," it means understanding from that deepest place within you, as opposed to, say, understanding it just intellectually.

Preacher

The term "preacher" will be used to refer to a person who conducts religious services in a church. While it may seem a bit outdated, it also seems to be the most universally acceptable term. Using the term pastor, priest, reverend, or minister, to name a few possibilities, could be indicative of a specific denomination and not be all-inclusive.

The Old and New Testament

The last terms I want to address are the Old Testament and the New Testament. Many Christians could be annoyed were I to say the "Christian Bible," when referring to the New Testament, or the "Hebrew Bible," when referring to the Old Testament. The Jewish religion, on the other hand, recognizes only those books included in the Old Testament, and this is important because Jesus was Jewish, and nothing that became new scripture would be written until decades after he died.

In fact, there could be no "new" testament without an "old" testament. One text is clearly built upon the other. Too often in modern, common understanding the New Testament is viewed as an evolved or updated theology that replaces the old—a new way to understand God that renders the old way obsolete.

"Testament" is another word for "covenant," which basically means an agreement. In the Old Testament, the original covenant was made when God chose the ancient Israelites as his people, and the agreement would be forever kept by their adherence to the Law of Moses.[1] In the New Testament,

---

1 The Torah—the first five books of the Old Testament.

the covenant is salvation offered to anyone through faith in Jesus Christ.

Jesus, however, certainly did not see the writings that came to be called the Old Testament as "old" scripture—to him it was simply the scripture, and he preached for it to be kept. In fact, Jesus said, "Do not think I have come to abolish the law or the prophets;[2] I have come not to abolish but to fulfill. For truly I tell you, until heaven and earth pass away, not one letter, not one stroke of a letter, will pass from the law until all is accomplished."[3]

It seems impossible to reference these books in a way that maintains their respective religious integrities and is also universally perceived as correct. It would, however, be too distracting and confusing to use names other than those by which they are generally known. Therefore, they will be referred to as the Old Testament and the New Testament.

The difficulties involved in arriving at universally acceptable terms relating to God should provide some insight into how little we actually know about God, which is comparable to the relatively few stars we can see in the night sky. When seeking to understand what we don't know about God, we are charting that infinitely vaster space we cannot see: the unknown.

---

2 "The law or the prophets" refers to the contents of the Hebrew Bible.
3 Matthew 5:17–18.

CHAPTER 3

THE UNKNOWN

From the moment human beings became self-aware on earth, questions arose that needed answering. We needed to somehow explain how life and the forces that kept it going came to be. Since prehistoric times, people believed in some idea of gods, or supreme beings, who created and watched over us, and with that belief came the need for a way to formalize the relationship between those beings and us, their people.

In the southeast Mediterranean region not far from where Christianity began, for well over three thousand years before Jesus was born, the Egyptian dynasties reigned over a religious civilization that believed various gods governed every facet of life, as well as the afterlife. People worshiped, prayed, and sacrificed to the gods for things like favorable weather for a good harvest, the well-being of their families, prosperity, curing the sick, childbirth, love, happiness, guidance through death, and the continuation of the soul in eternity—many of the same things people pray for today.

Just across the Mediterranean Sea to the northwest of the

Egyptians, for roughly eight hundred years before the time of Jesus, the ancient Greek civilization was flourishing. The Greeks, too, were polytheistic and practiced rituals involving offerings and animal sacrifice. Eventually the great Roman Empire conquered the entire region encompassing Egypt and Greece and assimilated many of their customs and religions.

While polytheism is no longer practiced much in the West, we have a lot else for which to thank those ancient cultures. While they, too, were influenced by those who came before and did not necessarily invent everything cited below, our culture has undeniably been greatly influenced by theirs.

The Egyptians had a structured civilization ruled by law and order. They had a writing system based on pictures (hieroglyphics). Ancient Greece gave us the concept of democracy and legislative structure, which evolved into the Roman senate for which ours is named. The alphabet and calendar we use today are closest to the Roman alphabet and calendar, both of which evolved from the Greek. All three civilizations had mathematics and medicine, irrigation systems, sophisticated architecture, literature, art, philosophy, theater, astronomy—on and on.

Today in the Western world, we look down on the polytheistic religions of the past. Despite their practitioners having had advanced civilizations and all they've contributed to us, we still believe that, in terms of their religions, the ancient polytheists got it wrong.

Some centuries prior to Jesus, in the land northeast of Egypt, Judaism developed into a major monotheistic religion. It centered on the worship of one God and living according to God's laws. Jesus grew up in this heritage and preached adherence to those laws, as well as his own new teachings he founded upon them. After he died, a new religion based on his life, works, teachings, death, and the belief in his resurrection began to emerge—Christianity. And over the centuries, it branched like a wild vine into a variety of forms.

Those people who lived a few thousand years ago were us. If you had lived in Rome two thousand years ago, chances are you would have held the same polytheistic beliefs as the rest of your people. You would have believed as you were raised to believe and what your culture dictated were the right beliefs to have. Conversely, if you transplanted a Roman baby into today's world, he too would likely have grown up holding the beliefs that were instilled in him in his youth.

Time laughs at those who believe they are as advanced as it gets. If the human race survives another thousand years, people will no doubt look back on us as no less naïve and misguided than we consider our ancestors to have been—or maybe even more so, as technology seems to evolve exponentially and often forces our beliefs to evolve as well. They will see that a great many of us were still plagued with fear when it came to God, and were most fearful of what happens to us when we die.

Many sermons I heard on Sunday perpetuated the fear of what would happen to us in the afterlife if we did not hold the right beliefs. Perhaps future students will learn this about us and feel the same way we do when we read that the elite of ancient Egypt placed jewelry, provisions, and scrolls in the tombs of their dead in order to assist them in the afterlife. Why are so many of us certain we're the ones who finally have the right answers?

Be it the polytheism of the Egyptians, Greeks, and Romans, or the monotheistic views widely held today, our religious beliefs have always been designed to answer fundamental questions about our existence. If you look closely though, God is not actually at the core of our religions. Religions evolved in response to our notions of God, but our notions about God evolved as our response to the unknown.

This is not to say that God did not already exist independent of our faith, but I'd be willing to bet that what we call God today is much closer to the God we created in response to the unknown than to the real whatever-whoever-God is.

When it comes to the subject of God or how we humans came to be, we don't know much more than those people did thousands of years ago. We have the same old questions: Did this world come to be as the result of a random chain of events or is there a creator? And, if the latter, who created the creator? Did the same creator create the sun and all the stars and planets in space? Where does space end? Sometimes we fool ourselves into believing we have the answers to these questions.

"Where does space end?"

"It doesn't. Space is infinite."

"Who created the world?"

"God did."

"Who created God?"

"God is infinite."

Our answers are just more questions in disguise.

In truth, we have very few answers to the fundamental questions of our existence. Medical science has come a long way and we know a great deal about the details of our bodies. We can routinely transplant organs, perform eye surgery with lasers, or unblock clogged arteries. Yet, within the mystery of how human life came to be, and all the forces governing it, there remain endless subdivisions of mysteries. How does the heart beat twenty-four hours a day for a lifetime? What governs the length of a lifetime (why do our cells last just so long)? How can we sleep on our side or hang upside down without having our organs smoosh together and stop? How exactly does memory work?

The simple answers are: circulation; human biology; synapses that fire in the mind. But these belie the underlying unknowns.

Does the heart drive circulation or does circulation drive the heart? Its perpetual motion alone is miraculous—unless you want to say it's ordinary. What is going on biologically when you want to recall the name of someone you met once ten years ago? Maybe you can't remember at first, but as you think, it's as if you are going through files in your mind, remembering back to where you were, what the circumstances were, digging deeper into details until after a long twenty seconds the name pops into your mind (or maybe you come so close but then it slips away). These are, of course, subjects it could take a whole book to address. I am a layman asking existential lay questions.

How do our minds not melt trying to understand the concept of a God?

Sometimes sanity itself seems like a gift we can easily take for granted. It allows us to live our lives rationally even though we can't comprehend how or why we exist. It allows us to accept God as an answer to the unknown. But sometimes sanity also allows us to take God and the perpetual miracle of our own lives for granted.

The breakneck pace of our modern world seems to leave little time to consider whether what we've been taught about God is true. It is more efficient to simply pay our dues by spending a short time in a house of worship once a week or on holidays than it is to take the long inward journey required to examine our own belief system.

Living in the present we are naturally aware of our advancement. We get in our car to drive somewhere at night and gaze at the array of lighted instruments and gauges on our dashboard that would have looked like the interior of a spaceship to someone living in the fifties. We can use an earpiece to speak on the telephone—no cords, no hands. We can even issue a voice command to "call Henry," and the phone obeys. We can ask our phone just about any factual question and it will answer. We have global positioning systems that allow us to navigate to an unknown destination. And all these technological wonders will be upgraded to stunning new heights every few years (in the years it took me to write this book I had to alter this paragraph multiple times to keep up with the changes).

Yet, when it comes to our religious beliefs, progress is deemed unnecessary because we accept without question that those beliefs are correct in every detail and that we should and must believe them. It is the only area of our lives where we cling to what people were thinking and believing two-or-more thousand years ago. Is that because we truly believe that every detail of our beliefs is correct, or because we are terrified of risking our souls by being wrong?

Ideally, religion is meant to help us find and develop a relationship with God. Shouldn't it, therefore, be helping us on our path toward learning more about God and providing us with spiritual understanding, so that we grow to understand ourselves and the world better with each passing day?

Many of us are fortunate enough to have our religion serve us in that way. Too often, however, just the opposite happens, despite our religious leaders' best intentions. Since ancient times we have been fixated on stories of the past because those stories are in the Bible and, as such, are part of our devotion— part of our worship. We see the Bible as a holy book, written by God, whose absolute truth must be accepted without question, which can cause us to overlook its plain practical value as a text for serving our spiritual development. As a result, we revere the Bible as a whole, but, ironically, because its words are said to be God's words, and therefore "beyond us," many of us are okay with not knowing more than a few sentences from it, as long as we know the general stories and what we need to believe.

Many of us believe those stories are factual and were dictated by God, despite the books in the Bible having numerous authors. Yet the stories and the words can be so difficult to understand at times, even contradictory, that what we really end up with as the "divine word" is whatever our religions have interpreted the Bible to mean.

Based on the belief that one God created all things, the

ancient Israelites decided how God wanted us to live, and then we subsequently decided what were or were not God's words ("we" meaning all who accept the Old Testament as, or part of, scripture). Eventually we made what we called God's laws. We claimed that we didn't create those laws or our beliefs about God—God told us what to believe and obey.

⚜⚜⚜⚜⚜

"In the beginning God created the heavens and the earth."[1] This God spoke only to a chosen few human beings on earth. He talked to Adam, Abraham, Moses, and a few others. There is no question of there being two distinct parties—God and whomever God spoke to. Moses found God high atop a mountain, where God spoke to him and gave him the Ten Commandments.

This God is separate from us.

We are separate from this God.

Throughout the Old Testament we are told this God must be feared. As mere human beings we must worship him and live by his commandments. It is not our place or within our capability to know the mind of God—much less to question him. If we break God's laws, the punishment would most often be death.

In the New Testament, we read about Jesus for the first time. Jesus is Jewish, he adheres to and preaches to keep God's laws, and he also emphasizes the value of love and how each and every individual could enter the kingdom of God.

---

1 Genesis 1:1.

Nowhere is this better exemplified than in a passage from the Gospel of Mark. A scribe asks Jesus, "Which commandment is the first of all?" Instead of quoting any one of the traditional commandments exactly, for example, "I am the Lord your God ... you shall have no other gods before me,"[2] Jesus gives a more elaborate reply, quoting another part of scripture, "The first is, 'Hear, O Israel: the Lord our God, the Lord is one; you shall love the Lord your God with all your heart, and with all your soul, and with all your mind, and with all your strength.'"[3]

Put more simply, the first commandment according to Jesus is to *love God*. In essence, his answer did not differ from the tradition that preceded him, but the choice of putting this answer in more clearly loving terms is no accident. It indicates an evolution in how we relate to God, but not a replacement— a progression of understanding. Isn't Jesus emphasizing a loving approach to our relationship with God, and doesn't it seem natural? Could it be that we are overdue for a more loving approach in our current religious understandings?

The second part of Jesus' answer to the scribe's question provides even more striking support for his emphasis on love. He goes on to say, "The second [commandment] is this, 'You shall love your neighbor as yourself.' There is no other commandment greater than these."[4]

Love your neighbor is among the most famous messages attributed to Jesus. While the statement could be called one of the pillars of his ministry, those words also come from the

---

2 Exodus 20:2.

3 Mark 12:29, which quotes Deuteronomy 6:4–5.

4 Mark 12:31. These two commandments are similarly said in Matthew 22:37–40 and Luke 10:27–28.

Old Testament.[1] His answer shows him maintaining the scripture while promoting a loving emphasis overall, and again, he chooses a verse of scripture that was not one of the traditional commandments.

It is an important point in our spiritual evolution that Jesus touched the lives of so many through love. People were able to feel the love of Spirit through Jesus. By learning about the love by which he lived and with which he treated almost everyone, including sinners, tax collectors, the sick, and the dying, Jesus gave people a way to feel the love of God. He led by the example of loving others, and, because of the many people who have followed his example, that love is still realized in the world today.

(However, I would be remiss if I did not acknowledge that for more than seventeen centuries, throughout the middle ages and still in places today, there have been those who somehow divorced Jesus from his loving words and examples he set and violently persecuted those who didn't believe as they do.)

As important as his preaching about loving others was Jesus' preaching that all people could find God. Much of his ministry, as told in the Gospels, involved his teaching people how to reach the kingdom of God. Yet, almost from the inception of Christianity, we chose to focus only on worshiping the divinity of Jesus Christ rather than on his teachings. We

---

1 "Do not seek revenge or bear a grudge against one of your people, but love your neighbor as yourself. I am the Lord" (Leviticus 19:18).

ignored Jesus' humanity and exalted him exclusively as the anointed one—the only one who could know God while alive, despite Jesus teaching us otherwise. We elevated and pushed him way up to the heavens—up, up, and away. And with that distancing came the fear of how to return to him someday.

We have so little about his life recorded, and yet we presume to know in detail about his lifelong character as a man. Most believers do not want to imagine Jesus as having been anything less than perfect; he was the one and only sinless man who ever lived.

If one day we unearthed an irrefutably legitimate, original Gospel that said Jesus as a young man had lived sinfully for many years before he began his ministry, would it change your opinion of him? If it said he sometimes liked to get drunk and tell tall tales would it lessen your respect for him and his words? This is not to suggest these things are true, it is to have you consider for a moment what criteria you use in valuating his words. It can be easy for us to accept his perfection and thereby just assume his words are perfect too—that is, our translation and interpretation of them, which can tempt us to avoid our own learning process as a means to appreciate and benefit from his wisdom and guidance.

The Bible has nothing to say about Jesus between the ages of roughly thirteen and thirty. We fill in the blank of that unknown with our own image of who Jesus was and had to be. He did live as a man after all—could not even the Son of God have been a regular guy who made mistakes or liked to goof around at times? Moving on, let's accept that Jesus was indeed perfect and sinless as a man, which is how I like to think of him. I don't try to know the unknowable unknown;

it's enough that the ideal gives me something to strive for, and regardless, I believe his instruction on how we should live and treat others, and the unlimited possibilities of our spiritual lives that he represents and teaches, are worthy enough gifts from the Bible.

Just as the acceptance of his perfection can cloud our objective learning process when it comes to his teachings, it seems the miracles of Jesus are often cherished far more than his words. How often are the miracles of Jesus cited as proof of his divinity? Ask yourself sincerely, if there were no miracles—if Jesus had never walked on water, made blind men see, or raised Lazarus from the dead—would your faith be the same? Would you still listen to what he had to say?

For many of us who believe in these wondrous stories, there is a temptation to then revere what he said as being God's holy words, yet remove them from the practical purpose Jesus intended them to have when he sought to teach others how to live righteously and grow spiritually.

Jesus shows us the way to go where he went and to know what he knew. But our own image of and ideas about him, based in large part on the miraculous stories of what he did and who he was, have left many of us so awestruck that we are unable hear his messages. If Jesus had given a sermon about how to be a good person and then walked on water before our eyes, do you think we'd remember the sermon? Of course, witnessing the miracle would be a blessed event that caused us to revere the divine being who created it. Yet surely we should also want to know everything that being had to say.

What people have seen in Jesus, from the time he lived to the present, is a light beaming like the sun. We feel its warmth, its love, and the spiritual truth that emanates from it. But the stories and accounts of the miracles he performed have helped to make his light shine so brightly that many of us drop to our knees in worship, believing that's all we mortals are meant to do.

Although Jesus beseeches all people to seek the Father, that search takes will, inner strength, and endurance, and so, many of us avoid walking that path and are only too happy to accept the fact that it is not our place to do so.

Instead, we worship the Son: He came; he knew God; he gave us everything we need to have spiritually. He gave us the gift of never having to search for spiritual answers, because he gave us all the answers that needed giving. All we have to do is believe in Jesus Christ as our Lord in order to be saved.

First, in the Old Testament, we had a God who existed on high—separate from us. Next, in the New Testament, the Lord descended to earth in human form, but in the end, he too was elevated and separated from us. Jesus now stands by God's right side in heaven, we are told, and if we hold the right beliefs and live the right life, we will join them after we die.

Separation from God became even more strongly accepted as our spiritual place.

CHAPTER 4

EGO

The Separate Being

Define ego.

Not so easy, is it?

Dictionaries commonly define ego as the self, as distinct from other selves in the world. Sometimes ego is defined as a sense of self-importance. One with a big ego has a strong sense of self. When one has an overdeveloped sense of self-importance, we call them egotistical, which is considered an insult to most people.

These characteristics do not, however, fully define the meaning of the word.

There is an underlying spiritual definition created by the belief that you are separate from God. Ego is the part of you that perceives yourself as outside of God.

Take the case we discussed at the end of the last chapter of those of us who are so in awe of the light emanating from

Jesus that we fall to our knees in worship and stop hearing what he has to tell us. The ego is the shadow created by the separation from that light, and that separation is a belief. Whether we say God, the Lord, or Yahweh, these words describe a supreme deity we look up to and worship as existing somewhere else.

The traditional understanding of ego we began this chapter with has common ground with the spiritual understanding of ego. If you don't believe in God, you perceive yourself as being alone, there is nothing more to you, and your ego is simply who you are, your *self*. The psychological implications of this belief, as pertains to your ego, are no different from believing in a God that is separate from you—in your thoughts or mental state you perceive yourself as alone.

This sense of being separate has nothing to do with whether you're surrounded by others, in love, in a relationship, or if you have family and friends you love and who love you, nor does it have anything to do with being lonely. It's a deeply internal belief, hidden from consciousness. Even if you have great faith in God, you might accept the fact that this life is not the time or place for you to be united with him. For now, you are an individual—"on your own"—and most of us identify ourselves this way. Together, we constitute an ego-dominated world.

A sense of one's own self-importance is not something we commonly associate with spirituality; the ego is not commonly defined in relation to God.

In an ego-dominated world, instead of saying, "That guy has a big ego," it may sound silly to say, "That guy has a powerfully fortified illusion of being separate," yet it is the more precise truth.

The brief look at the ego we are having here will be essential to have had when we get to Part Two, which is devoted to Jesus' words in the Bible, because, as you will see, there are times our ego plays a part in our understandings of those words.

All of the descriptions of people that I use as examples in the following sections are broad generalizations used only for the purpose of identifying the ego. Obviously no two people are the same, we humans are far too complex to be defined by a particular label, and our individualities are too numerous to categorize. I can only provide examples based on my own life experience, which may be very different from yours, even though the ego itself is a universally human characteristic.

Birth of the Ego

As we progress from childhood to adulthood, what is said to us can sometimes affect us as much as what happens to us. We might hear the same things as a child that we hear as an adult, but while adults can choose to keep what serves them and reject what does not, for a child each word is like planting a seed in the soil of who we will become.

As a child we begin to ask questions. The first answers we receive typically come from our parents or whomever raises us. When it comes to questions about who or what is God, they might pass on the answers they were taught by their religion, or whomever raised them, which we then internalize as part of who we are. If such was their religion, they were who first taught us there is a God in heaven, ruling over our life here on earth, and if we believe certain things and behave in certain ways, we will get to be with God in heaven when we die.

A child's mind is not developed enough to understand the ramifications of such profound concepts. On a soul level, however, children know a great deal. When we are taught that we are separate from God, there is a powerful latent result: An ego is born.

The Bible tells us that Adam and Eve fell from grace, taking the human race down with them for all time. This is a good allegorical way to look at ego; from a spiritual perspective, we are born alone in this world. We are separate from the start.

The ego develops from any perceived separation. A child obviously does not need to think about God in order to form an ego. At some point when you were very young, you became aware of your thoughts and began to think of yourself as being internally alone. Maybe it happened when you were lying in bed at night staring at the ceiling. Perhaps it was on your first day at school—away from your parents and thrust into an environment full of strangers. You began an inner dialogue that continues to this day.

That first awareness of self is like finding yourself alone in a foreign land. You feel vulnerable, which instinctively triggers you to start developing a way to protect yourself. When you were lying in your bed at night as a child, that first awareness of yourself may have been experienced as your first fear—fear of the dark. *What is that shape across the room? Are there monsters in the closet or under the bed?* Maybe your young ego found a solution in using a nightlight, which banished the darkness and reminded you that you were in your safe warm room with a parent not far away. Perhaps when you went to school for the first time and felt isolated among strangers, you looked at a bunch of kids talking in a group and thought, *How do they know each other already?* or *Who will I be friends with?* And maybe you soon found that when you made a new friend or two, you began to feel more at ease because you no longer felt isolated. Or, if you were self-confident, that grew stronger with more friends.

The core belief that you are separate and alone generates all kinds of vulnerabilities, which in turn spin more self-protective thoughts. This develops into a belief system that dominates your inner dialogue, as you form your sense of who you are. This sense of who you are is your ego, and it takes on a life of its own. This is the separate being inside you. As a child you are not going to have the conscious thought, *I am separate*, but this inner belief still manifests in your thoughts, behavior, and what you say.

Since your ego is part of you, it shares your impulse to survive; the ego wants to live. It must guard your vulnerable self in order to guard itself—to ensure its own survival by serving a purpose that is essential to you. It must preserve your identity as a separate being. One of the tools the ego uses for this is, paradoxically, fitting in. How you look to others becomes an important issue. If you stand out in some unusual way, rather than remain anonymous, you may be attacked. It might be only a verbal assault, but words can hurt—they can elicit distress and rock the ego's stable world.

Take, for example, what can happen on an elementary school playground. Even in the society of children, there is a common understanding of what is "cool" and what is not, especially in terms of style. If, for example, a boy dresses differently from everyone else or can't afford the same clothes or shoes, he might be teased or bullied or even simply ignored.

Those who have the "right" clothes probably feel secure, while the one who is ridiculed is likely to feel awful and alone. Maybe he will cry and some of his pain will be released. Or perhaps *he* will become the bully as a way to deflect from feeling uncomfortable. Or he might simply put a brave face on things, in order to protect himself and, of course, his ego.

The children who feel superior, on the other hand, also feed their egos, but their sense of superiority is simply separation by another name. They separate themselves from the one kid who doesn't conform, and also prove the vulnerability of their situation by depending on allies for support. Their sense of superiority could be lost in a moment if their circumstances were to change. Whatever our circumstances happen to be, our ego's only concern is that we identify ourself as a separate being, which insures its own safety.

Adolescence

By the time many of us reach adolescence, we have accepted that, on the soul level, we are alone. Our thoughts based on this belief have grown powerful. They run wild and make a lot of noise, and we may live many years believing that noise is who we are.

Our ego continues its mission to protect itself by protecting us. It does not want us to question who we are. If we feel alone, sad, or unsatisfied, we might start poking around inside our head to find out why. If, in doing that, we became aware of the separate being inside us and how it was causing us to think, we might start to address the fact that we have an ego. We might want to be rid of it. Introspection is therefore a threat to our ego. And so, it keeps our attention turned outward as it continues driving us to adapt and blend into our environment.

Do you remember your high school days? You may have been even more concerned with fitting in than when you were younger, and better at achieving it. You could pick something you liked to do and derive the dual benefit of also fitting in. In my high school, if you were a guy, you might have played sports. If you were not athletic, perhaps you fit in with those who shared a love of video games, movies, comics, or chess, or with others in band or orchestra. Some teens found their place with a group of kids who smoked, drank, did drugs, or committed petty crimes for kicks. American adolescence is a time of cliques—groups of peers with shared interests.[1]

The exceptional athletes (the school jocks) were probably popular and got the pretty girls. It might seem that these boys were anything but anonymous. However, we are talking about a system of ego, and in terms of ego, they were the stars of the already accepted standard of "normal." They not only met the minimum fitting-in requirement of the ego, but by excelling, they solidified their position within the system. In essence, they rode on the shoulders of all the other members of that

---

1 Of course these generalizations can't cover all the reasons why kids hang out together. And some kids were naturally introverted, more isolated, and didn't "fit in" for other reasons. This is a category I fell into.

system—to cheers and admiration. The status they achieved made their egos (their self-identity) that much stronger. They were kings for the day in the ego realm.

If you were a girl, same principle. If you were athletic, you might have naturally bonded with other athletic girls through sports. If you were quiet, perhaps you'd have been most comfortable with other quiet girls. Like the boys, you had the band, orchestra, debate team, or other types of clubs to feel at home in. Or perhaps you hung out with girls who smoked behind the school, or drank and partied.

There were exceptional girls too, although the criteria might have been different from those of the boys'. In my school, the exceptional girls were usually the prettiest ones. Some of them were cheerleaders and stayed connected to their exceptional male counterparts. They were "popular" and hung out with other popular girls. They not only fit in but had the boys fawning over them to let them know they were special. They too, being stars in the system, had their egos inflated and strengthened. They were queens for the day in the ego realm.

These observations of boys and girls are based entirely on the reality of what I experienced in my own school's system of ego. They are not intended to be statements or definitions of what made someone actually exceptional, nor do they necessarily make logical sense. Sure, a handsome jock might have been the king of the prom. However, in the egoic hierarchy of my high school tribe, athletic talent trumped looks for males while, for females, looks trumped athletic talent. To a large degree, doesn't that same attitude persist through adulthood in our culture?

All the different ways kids try to fit in are manifestations of their egos seeking security. One of the reasons cliques develop is because there is strength in numbers; the more you are like the others in your group, the less you stand out.

Trappings of the Ego

The years after high school are a period of transition into adulthood. Whether we go to college, join the workforce, or enter the armed forces, by the time we are a young adult, our ego is highly developed. It is running our life: making our decisions, governing how we feel, telling us how to interpret what happens to us, telling us what is valuable, telling us what success is. Over the years it has become more adept at protecting itself.

As an ego-dominated being, we don't know any other way than to identify with this independent self of ours. Maintaining our peace of mind can be challenging. It seems we are always a victim of whatever adversity life throws at us, and that our mental state and emotions are dependent on our circumstances. We may believe in God, go to a house of worship regularly, and pray, but God is still up there somewhere, while we are down here on our own. A few of us are born into money, which can cushion us from some of life's adversities, but most of us need to fend for ourselves— psychologically, spiritually, and economically.

From the ego's perspective, we are standing outside in the cold, alone and shivering. This is not a state we wish to be in; it feels uncomfortable. We have real needs. We need a place to live, food, water, clothes, insurances, a car to drive. Money will buy us these things. While they serve our survival, they also serve the ego by keeping us stable—keeping it okay to be living "alone" or separate.

One of the most important choices ego has to make for us is how to earn the money we need. Because we live in an ego-dominated society, our ego might look at the end goal (money) and works backwards to determine what to do with our life. Generally, as a young adult, we pick something we like, or are good at, that will pay the bills. This not only makes life more enjoyable, it also helps us fit into society.

Someone who has a big ego may not be content to just pay the bills and will desire riches. This would not be an arbitrary desire. The ego seeks invincibility, and while paying the bills may provide our basic needs, it still leaves the ego in a precarious position. What would happen if we lost our job? What would happen if something went wrong? Where would the ego be then? If some tragedy were to befall us and we were left with no money, we might be deeply afraid. All discomfort and fear lead us back to poking around inside our head and asking questions. Questioning leaves the ego open to exposure, and so it must prevent that by providing for our comfort. The ego wants ultimate security, which it can think comes with a lot of money.

This is not to say pursuing riches is always ego driven; financial security is a real need, and riches can make life very pleasurable. On another note, having a lot of money (success to many) is the adult version of high school stardom. While the pursuit of riches might not have been his goal in life, the high school "nerd" who pulls up to his twentieth high-school reunion in a Lamborghini might just be crowned the new king.

The Mature Ego

Your ego wants you to feel good and complete with it at the helm. Its job is done to perfection when you are unaware that it is in control—or that it even exists. Your ego is most secure when you believe it is simply you.

As an example of how this works (this could apply to any number of people or types), let's say a woman is getting dressed for work. She stands in front of a full-length mirror, turns slightly each way and thinks, *Do I look good? Does this outfit work?* If asked why she had these thoughts, she might say something like, "I just happen to care about how I look." However, underlying that reasoning is the ego, which has a different agenda. The ego is thinking, *How will I look to others? Will others think I am good-looking?* It is critical for the ego to be accepted by others in order to fit in. If she stands out in a way that draws negative attention, she will be vulnerable. If she see others whispering or making fun of her, she might feel terrible and start looking inward for protection. She might subconsciously begin to detect flaws in her ego-system of thought and search for ways of thinking that are more conducive to her well-being, which would put the ego in jeopardy.

If, on the other hand, she happens to be particularly good-looking, she will also stand out, but in the best possible way for her ego. She will not only meet but exceed the criteria for fitting in. She will be admired by those around her, and her separate being will be strengthened. Even if she receives negative attention from those who are jealous, that too will serve to strengthen her sense of self—because, after all, it is her good looks that caused the jealousy. These are reasons why beautiful women and handsome men often have big egos.

Good looks, however, can also backfire. Some might automatically assume that because a woman is beautiful she can't also be intelligent, or that a handsome man must have had an easy time becoming successful. These (potentially erroneous but stereotypical) judgments can be upsetting, so once again that person's ego would have to figure out a way to deal with those feelings. In each of these scenarios, the ego reacts to how the person is viewed by others. Whether those views are positive or negative, the ego must keep them psychologically secure.

Any time our insecurities are brought to our attention, the ego must fight to maintain its security, which depends on our having peace of mind. From the ego's perspective, the only solution is a stronger ego. But at some point these battles become tiresome. Maybe we're tired of caring so much about how we look to others, not just physically but in all aspects of our life—our job, career status, how much money we have, our relationships. Maybe we're just exhausted from having to think so much at all.

Perhaps we then begin to pray, meditate, or read books on self-improvement, because we've heard there might be a better way (we know inherently there is a better way). We start to pay more attention to our thoughts—to why we think and behave in the ways we do, to how we're reacting to situations—we start to examine ourselves with less ego involvement. This, in turn, begins to free us from the dominant hold our egos have over us.

CHAPTER 5

BREAKING THE EGO

The first step in breaking the pattern of egoic thought and behavior is, of course, awareness of having an ego. It is difficult to view ourselves objectively. Our thoughts can be so familiar to us that we don't commonly observe them. We don't think to think of our thoughts as thoughts. For example, someone rubs us the wrong way and we immediately think, *I can't stand that person*, but maybe we don't dig deeper to discover the source of our animosity. Our ego is quick to react. But every once in a while, we have a moment of clarity—we realize we are the thinker of our thoughts. We can then choose what we think.

Can you recall a time when you first met someone and after they said just a few words you made a sweeping judgment of them and decided you didn't like them, but then stopped yourself in amazement? *Why did I just think that?* Perhaps there's a person who became a dear part of your life because you chose that awareness, and years later you both had a good laugh about it (turns out they didn't like you either).

Imagine, for example, there is a man who is at some social

function, in a small circle of people talking, and someone he barely knows comments, "If you have faith in God anything is possible—he can make you overflow with abundance or heal any illness." This really grates on his nerves. He believes in God, but he thinks this is just the kind of flippant, spiritual babble that sounds good but has no basis in reality. Besides, it sounds like using God for selfish purposes. He immediately begins to make further assumptions about the person. He finds himself getting angry. Then he realizes how ridiculous he's being, getting so wound up over nothing. He looks back at the same person (who is still talking) and thinks, *This guy isn't so bad. What's the matter with me?*

Times like this, when we can interrupt our automatic patterns and look at ourselves objectively, are a blessing. What happened in the case above had nothing to do with the speaker of the words; it had to do with the words and what they meant to the man hearing them. Internally, the words indicated that he didn't understand something. Since he didn't know if it was true that with faith in God anything is possible, he took the words to mean, "You don't really know God," or "You have some lack of knowledge," and that brought up a wave of insecurity.

Implying he doesn't know God might lead to thoughts that cause him to seek further spiritual counsel, which could lead him to question what he knows. That might cause him to ask one of the most threatening questions to the ego: *Do I know God?* That question in turn could lead to a loosening of the ego's powerful hold on him, because it could lead him to start praying more earnestly to God for better answers, or lead him to meditate, or perhaps to go to some type of self-help seminar, any of which means he'd be humbling himself to some degree and not solely serving the ego, which would potentially allow him to learn something new. He might start seeking out literature in new spiritual areas, or begin to suspect that he needs not be or feel separate. He might even start having faith that greater things *are* possible with God.

In seeking to understand ourselves and God better, we threaten our identity as a separate being. Our ego, therefore, defends itself by blocking out the intruding thought. Perhaps later, when the man reflects on what was said that bothered him, he will get bothered again and reinforce his initial reaction by remembering a lifetime of what's been said to him by preachers, family, friends—anyone—that have led him to believe that the guy at the party was wrong.

If he were to remember that it says in the Gospels, "with God all things are possible,"[1] no problem; the ego will remind him that those words applied only to Jesus, because only Jesus was one with God. There is no foe more wily than a threatened ego.

It's become fairly common knowledge that often when we are thinking non-loving thoughts (such as the ones the man had about the stranger speaking about God), the reason for those thoughts lies in the distant past. Let's say, for example, a little boy got stuck high up in a tree for several hours until someone finally rescued him. Now, as an adult, his thought patterns protect him from repeating that traumatic event. If someone asks him to go hiking up a mountain, his immediate response is to think, *I don't enjoy hiking up mountains*, although he may have no conscious recollection of the event underlying that

---

1 Matthew 19:26; Mark 10:27; Luke 18:27.

thought. Most of us have automatic reactions that are triggered in particular situations, and usually if it's a strong reaction we can trace it deeply within, often to our childhood.

The man's anger with the person who is talking about faith's yielding worldly rewards came from his ego. To his ego, the other person speaks heresy because he speaks about knowing God, which the man had been taught since childhood is not his place to do. He speaks a language opposing separation from God. Therefore, he is the enemy. Fortunately, the man listening has a big heart (as I believe most of us do) and can override his ego's insecurity. He may not be able to agree with what the other man said, but he can love him anyway, or at least not hate him.

You'd think it would be a wonderful thing to find God. If it is true that anything is possible with God, it would seem to be to our greatest benefit to move closer to God every day. Then why do we not abandon the ego immediately? Because, even though it might be wise for us to break free of its hold, the ego has been with us our whole life. It wants to live and will do anything in its power to survive. Just as an animal with a wounded paw might become ferocious to protect itself, the ego may rise in its own defense when challenged. And yet, those challenges are often the opportunities for growth and finding better ways of thinking or behaving.

The Wounded Ego

Were you ever in a great mood for no apparent reason? Maybe you were doing the dishes or vacuuming the rug and just felt good. Then someone said something unpleasant to you. Maybe someone told you that it looks as if you've put on a few pounds. Or maybe you forgot to do something and your spouse called you irresponsible. You don't feel good anymore, and, as time goes by, your mind keeps gnawing away at the insult and you feel worse and worse.

First you feel angry that you've been treated poorly. Next, you begin to think that the insult actually had some merit and you feel bad about yourself. These are manipulations of the ego. It doesn't want you to figure out that there is any difference between your ego and yourself because that threatens its control. It wants you to think you are under attack, rather than make the distinction that your negative feelings are coming from your ego—that your ego feels attacked. Your ego wants someone to blame (you or the other person) for being flawed, in order to distract you from realizing that only you can choose how you will interpret and feel about events. And so, it makes you feel lousy about the other person or lousy about yourself. Your ego doesn't care whether you suffer— only that it is safe, with your attention turned away from it.

We can, however, learn powerful lessons from things that shake us up, if we only do exactly what the ego does not want us to: get to the bottom of it. First we must figure out why we could go from feeling so good to so bad in an instant. If our mood can change that easily, it is not because of what someone said to us, but because of the weakness of our own foundation, which crumbles as a result.

Let's say it is some young woman's dream to be an actress. Call her Julie and place her in a New York City suburb. Julie lives with her parents while going to acting school. She acts in community theater productions while working as a waitress to cover her expenses. One day, she finally lands a small role with a few lines in an off-Broadway show. With tears of joy, she calls her friends to share the news in such exhilaration they can barely make out what she's saying. She is glowing all the way home on the train. She thinks, *I'm finally making it. My dreams are coming true.*

She runs into the house to tell her mother how well the audition went. But her mother, who has never been happy with her daughter's "unrealistic pursuit" of an acting career, just rolls her eyes and says, "But you're a waitress." Almost instantly, Julie's elation turns to despair. She runs to her room and weeps uncontrollably.

What happened?

Once Julie is behind the closed bedroom door, head buried in the safety of her favorite pillow, there are two ways her mind can go.

One way is into defense mode. "Mom is such a bitch. She's jealous of me for fulfilling my dreams because she never fulfilled hers. She doesn't understand me at all. I'm talented. The people at the audition saw that. I'm not going to let her do this to me. I'm better than this. I know better." She dries her tears and finds strength in who she is—a talented actress who just landed a part. Then she calls her best friend, who can commiserate and give support.

In this scenario, Julie rallied to overcome a particular incident. But is she really any the wiser? She has certainly addressed the symptoms—her anger and emotional distress— and is successful this time, but will she be the next time? She's like a person with a cough who swallows cough medicine; the symptom is quelled, but the disease is not cured. Julie has not yet found the root cause of her distress, so whatever it is still lies dormant and ready to flare up again when the right trigger comes along. Since her coping mechanism worked to overcome her distress, that might become the way she continues to deal with this problem. If her mother's disapproval continues to trigger her loss of composure and confidence in herself, she must either find the root cause in order to remedy it or stay away from the trigger. If she fails to fulfill her dream of becoming a successful actress, what started out as resentment of her mother could easily turn to blaming her for not being more supportive. Perhaps, sadly, the two will grow further apart.

While Julie suffers, however, someone else is celebrating a victory. Someone else just went, *phew, tragedy averted!* That someone is her ego. At the moment her mother declared "but you're a waitress," Julie lost faith in her own identity as an actress. That was the root cause of her distress. She had identified with, and been bolstered by, her success at the audition. Her ego had freshly defined her as a talented actress, confirmed in the eyes of others, and on the right career path.

Based on nothing more than ephemeral circumstantial evidence, Julie had identified with the person the world told her she was. But because of that, when her mother then saw her in a different light, Julie instantly doubted herself. As a separate being, she was exposed and vulnerable—caught between two pieces of evidence and not knowing which told the truth of who she was—an actress or a waitress. As she fell into a morass of distress, panic, and tears, her ego fought valiantly in its own defense—it retook the helm.

But what if, instead of going into defense mode, Julie had become introspective? What if she asked herself, "How did this just happen? Yes, Mom is Mom, but this is my problem. How can I be so sure of myself and then completely lose it like that in a moment? And why can't I let it go? Am I just a waitress? Who am I?"

Ah. The blessed question of questions. The gateway to truth and self-understanding.

Identity

"Who am I?" With honesty and grit, Julie asks the tough question, "Am I just a waitress? Am I simply a product of my circumstances, raised here in this town, the result of my upbringing—my parents and school—all leading up to my job as a waitress? Am I just Julie? Is there nothing more to me?"

She sits for a moment, curious and reflective but almost resigned to her lack of understanding. Then, another voice comes into her head. There is an answer coming. "I know there is more to me than this. All the circumstances of my life are true, and who I have become as a result of them is true. I am, in reality, a waitress, yet there is a part of me that is much more. I feel love and a profound sense of knowledge that seems to transcend my age; I feel my soul. My soul knows more than my chattering mind can ever know. What my soul has learned is for keeps and is somehow the real me.

"There have been moments when I was acting that I felt myself being taken over by the character I played. I would start out self-conscious, but as I let myself just be, the character seemed to live through me. I seemed to become a vessel for something greater than myself. What they didn't teach me about in acting school is that the more I am able to let go and stay in moments like these, the better I become as an actress.

"When I first started out in acting, those moments would come and I would think what a great actress I was, at which point the magic would disappear. I would forget a line or become myself again, and everyone would see it happening. Wow. Half of acting is the Zen art of surrendering and allowing something greater to flow through me. When I am able to do that I am something more—I am a soul, I am spirit. I am not just a product of circumstance. I am the true me.

"So why did I get so thrown when Mom said that? I see now it was because I didn't know who I really am. Her saying I was just a waitress triggered a lifetime of self-doubt. I felt sad and distressed because I was terrified she might be right. But I see now that I am much more. I feel such powerful love coming through me right now. *What is this?* Is this God?

"And poor Mom—this has been a tough time for her, too. She and Dad paid a lot of money to get me through college, and here I am a few years later, still working as a waitress and living at home. She hasn't had an easy life either. Grandma was ten times harder on her than she's ever been on me. She wasn't even allowed to consider her dreams. It was just marriage, kids, end of story. I love Mom."

Julie then goes down to the kitchen and gives her mother a big hug. Her mother collapses in her arms and says, "I'm sorry, baby. I'm so sorry." In that moment they are closer than they've ever been before.

Spirit channels love. Ego channels fear.

Who are you? Are you a product of circumstance? Does everything from your childhood define who you are—how you were raised, how loving your parents were, how much money you had? What about any suffering you had—maybe some traumatic experience—does that tell you who you are? How about your current life: What do you do for a living, how successful are you, how much money do you have? Are you married? Do you have children? Where do you live? Do any of these circumstances wholly define who you are?

Asking these kinds of questions is our first step toward awakened spirituality (spiritual-reality). Before we can discover who we are, we may have to learn who we are not. If we are an ego-dominated being, as most of us are, we won't be able to fully discover who else we might be until we first realize we have an ego and understand what it is. But if we take the time, we can trace every aspect of ourselves back to its roots, many of them to the soil of our childhood, and learn how we came to be who we are in all facets, overturning stones that few of us come to know are even there for our whole lives.

Having done that, we discover we are much more than a product of the circumstances of our life. And once we start to realize who we truly are, the days are numbered for the reign of our ego. Chances are, having been dominated by it for so long, it will be difficult to eliminate our ego altogether. We can't all meditate in the mountains for twenty years, or go out to the desert and fast for forty days. We can, however, admit we are egoholics. We can smile to ourselves and say, "My name is _____, and I have a big ego."

Ready to Move On

Do you think I am somewhere else? Do you
think, "God is in heaven, but I am down here
on earth"? I would rather you know me than
believe in me. What is the truth of your
heart—do you feel separate from me?

If all or most of the time you feel separate from God, you
are governed by ego, as most of us are. But don't worry. To
learn such a truth is a grand blessing. You have taken your
place among the rare pioneers of Spirit. You have found the
door. You stand on the threshold of the realm of Spirit.

You are a spiritual being. It doesn't matter whether or not
you know it or believe it. Whether or not you were introduced
to God as a child, your soul longs to know the truth about
God. You can hear about God ten thousand times and develop a blind faith as mighty as a mountain. Or you can deny
there is a God and develop a blind lack of faith as mighty as
a mountain. Either way, at the core of your being, there is a
spiritual question you will continue to ask throughout your
life: "Is God real?"

This question is asked in many different ways: "Am I
alone?" "Is Spirit real?" "Do I have a soul?" "Does God know
who I am?" "Will I go somewhere after I die?" "Is there any
more to this life than meets the eye; are there forces at play of
which I'm unaware?" "Does God know I have bills to pay?"

You enter this life with a seemingly blank slate. You probably don't remember anything about your life before the age

of three or four. For many years you have no intimate knowledge of anything beyond yourself (no spiritual knowledge of anything beyond your self). The question of whether or not you are alone persists, and there are only two possible answers: Spirit or ego; love or fear. There is a God with you, or there is not. The fear of being alone, on a soul level, is universally human. Most of us don't want to be alone, and of course having a mate, family, or friends we love and who love us can solve that. But at the same time, other people are not required for us to know we are never alone.

If we accept on the level of our soul not only that God is real, but also that we are never spiritually alone (that God is truly with us), we will have a great sense of comfort. At this time, however, the world we live in is dominated by ego-minded people. Spiritually speaking, that means most of us believe we are removed from God, which can make the path of staying aware of God, or of our spirit, more challenging. We might have had some spiritual experiences, but we haven't learned how to live in consistent spiritual awareness. Both spiritually and in reality, the ego dominates our life.

If you look into your psyche and find *There is just me here, nothing more; God is real, but I am alone while on this earth*, your identity as a separate being seems natural. This is the delusion, and it is a powerful one. It is omni-seductive. It meshes perfectly with the belief that you can't really know God personally. The ego will vehemently fight to maintain that delusion.

Does the ego truly care about your well-being?

No; its self-preservation is more important than your happiness.

As we now move forward into Part Two and delve into the meaning of Jesus' words, this knowledge and awareness of the ego will be of vital importance. If we are presented with information that pertains to our beliefs, especially if it is new to us or from a source with which we are unfamiliar, there is always the chance our ego will be triggered to defend itself. If at any turn it suspects that something conflicts (or even *might* conflict) with our beliefs, it snaps into action in order to self-protect, and that can take the form of our being easily affronted. We can be quick to reject new information because we are suddenly out of our comfort zone, but often growth, or even revelation, is awaiting us on the other side of that discomfort. I ask you please to stay vigilant and not jump to any conclusions about what this book will ultimately have to say before you've finished it.

It might be impossible to write a book that discusses religion without offending *someone*, or without creating some controversy, but one thing I can promise you: There is love behind every word you will read.

Over these next few chapters, we will explore all of Jesus' messages that pertain to hell and determine whether they are in harmony with our common understandings of them. Some of those understandings came into being long after Jesus died and have gone unquestioned by a great many of us to this day.

If you have a passion for studying the Bible, I believe you'll find this next section to be nourishing and enthralling. But, if studying the Bible is just not your thing, I recommend that you try to stick with this by taking in one small section at a time, at whatever pace works for you. It is here that any fears you may have about hell will be removed, because you will know for yourself what Jesus actually said about it. Also, the following chapters will give you powerful biblical support to be well-primed for what comes in Part Three, which is more purely spiritual.

Now let's get down to business...

PART II

CHAPTER 6
THE DOCTRINE OF FEAR

As you read in the Introduction, this book was inspired by an experience I had when a voice spoke to my thoughts and addressed troubling questions I had about the religious beliefs I'd heard taught for many years. The chapters in this section are the result of thousands of hours I spent over a few years studying and researching the Bible, as I sought to either corroborate or refute the messages I had received.

I have continued, where it seemed called for, to quote the voice as it spoke directly to me, in order that it might also speak directly to you. If the words do not speak directly to your own religious experience, or if you are not Christian or don't believe in God, perhaps the words will still provide you with new ways of looking at your own long-held beliefs.

In the Introduction, I said the voice spoke as God, a guide, a friend, or as Spirit itself. For that reason, sometimes it spoke in the first person ("I" or "me"), and sometimes in the third person ("God"). While this was not confusing for me at the time, I could see where it might be confusing for someone to read if I didn't mention it here. It's become clearer to me over time that certain messages were better served when relayed in the more objective sense of the third person, and I also didn't want to change the original words I had written down.

Most people who believe in God believe that God is good—God is Love. You would think that religious systems, which worship God, would also maintain that belief. Unfortunately, because of the influence of the human ego, your belief system developed with a dark side. Isn't that natural? Ego is the assertion of self outside of God.

Your belief system has two sides that cannot be separated. One side contains all the love and spiritual guidance passed on by the one you call Jesus Christ, which can bring you to God. The dark flip side is all about fear—that you cannot know or ever be with God if you don't accept Jesus Christ as the Lord and your Savior. Through this paradigm, your life on earth has been deemed a trial of faith with eternal ramifications.

What happens after death has always been one of humanity's ultimate fears. You were offered a way to alleviate that fear with the promise of eternal salvation (heaven), but were also threatened with a more dreadful fear—eternal damnation (hell).

Spiritual bullies—those who command you to believe as they believe and not to question what you are told—have sought to impose this ideology on you since its inception. However, you may not recognize the latest evolution of their methods. Though the days of bloody proselytizing are over and people are no longer burned at the stake for denying Jesus, the core spiritual belief is still the same: believe or burn—a doctrine of fear.

The entirety of the Gospels—the entire Good News—has been reduced to: you will go to heaven if you believe in the Lord Jesus Christ, which is especially good news based on the alternative you've been given.[1]

Hell

Scripture is often cited to support the existence of hell. Yet, when I took the time to examine the scriptures, I found disparities between what the Bible says about hell and what I had been taught about hell.

---

1 The English word "gospel" is derived from the Old English word "godspell," which is a translation of the Greek word for "good news" that appeared in the original Greek language of the New Testament manuscripts. Hence, gospel=good news.

Chief among these disparities was the main reason you would end up in hell: for not believing in Jesus Christ. Yet you will not find that stated or expounded upon by Jesus in any of the Gospels. If such had been his intention, perhaps there would have been another set of books called "the bad news."

In the Gospels, Jesus did use a word that came to be translated as "hell" in most of our English Bibles. However, the term he used does not mean what most people think of as hell. In addition, and more importantly, the reasons for you going to the place Jesus spoke about were not based on any of your beliefs about him. I will show this through scripture.

Every time we see Jesus use the word hell in the Gospels it is a translation of the Greek word *Gehenna*, and in most modern English translations of the New Testament, you will see a footnote telling you that.[1] Therefore, one of the first questions we need to ask is, "What did Jesus mean when he used the word *Gehenna?*"

Gehenna is the Greek version of the Hebrew name for a real valley *(Ge-Hinnom)* outside of ancient Jerusalem. Since the Old Testament was originally written in Hebrew, the name appears in most English versions of the Old Testament as the valley "of Hinnom," or "of the son of Hinnom," because the valley was owned by the family of Hinnom. It is still there today (you can take a guided tour of it).

The valley is mentioned eleven times in the Old Testament. Three of those times it appears mundanely in a paragraph

---

1 Including the *NRSV (New Revised Standard Version), NIV (New International Version), NKJV (New King James Version), ASV (American Standard Version), ESV (English Standard Version), HCSB (Holman Christian Standard Bible), NASB (New American Standard Bible), ISV (International Standard Version).*

describing the geography of the region ('there's a hill over there, the valley of Hinnom next to it, a town south of that, etc.').[2] The other eight times speak of it as a place where children were sacrificed by fire to the pagan god Molech.[3] God expressly forbids people to partake in the practice (upon penalty of death).[4] The valley, therefore, in its association with idolatrous and abominable practices, became a desecrated place in Israel.

It is clear from the use of the name *Gehenna* in the New Testament that the reference was carried forward in Jewish culture to the times when Jesus lived. The association of *Gehenna* with fire is found multiple times in the Gospels of Mark and Matthew, and the association of fire with hell has been with us ever since.

So, did Jesus use *Gehenna* to refer *literally* to a desecrated place we would not want our body to be thrown into or buried in? Did he use its fire as a *metaphor* to refer to the suffering we would incur if we lived a life of sin? Or did he use it as a *symbol* for a place of eternal fire to which God could send us upon judgment? Most of us were told of another option: that "hell" *(Gehenna)* in our Bibles is the name of an actual place of eternal torment, existing in another dimension (or, as some believe, in the great depths of the earth), where we could go after we die. As the doctrine of fear states: believe or burn.

Since *Gehenna* in the Bible refers to a real place outside Jerusalem, and we define our word "hell" as an afterlife place existing in another dimension (or deep in the earth), our word

---

2 Joshua 15:8, 18:16; Nehemiah 11:30.

3 2 Chronicles 28:3, 33:6; 2 Kings 23:10; Jeremiah 7:31–32, 19:2,6; 32:35.

4 Leviticus 20:2; Jeremiah 7:30–34.

"hell" is therefore a mistranslation of *Gehenna*. In these next few chapters, we will see even more compelling reasons why Jesus' use of *Gehenna* is not the same as our hell.

This can be shocking when we learn it for the first time (it certainly was for me). Yet it is here we must begin if we are to ascertain what Jesus said and meant when he used the word *Gehenna*. We need to go through the easier task of proving what it did *not* mean to him.

The Twelve Verses that Refer to Gehenna

In the first centuries of what came to be your current belief system, those who created it used scripture to establish that hell existed, and then leveraged the threat of hell against you if you didn't accept all of their interpretations of scripture, which took precedence over the actual words.

Somewhere along the way, a leap was made from scripture, and hell became the place you go if you don't accept Jesus Christ as your Savior. Every mention of hell in the Bible was then given this meaning, despite what the verses actually said.

We will start by going through all the verses in which "hell" is specifically written in the English New Testaments we most widely use,[1] and because in almost every instance it is a mistranslation of the word *Gehenna*, I will use that correct word in the verses and in reference, as it is seen in the original Greek language of the New Testament.[2] As we look at these verses, we will also see the reasons Jesus gave for why we could possibly end up there.

It is all too easy to keep repeating the same few verses about *Gehenna* and make it seem as if the Bible is filled with such verses. It is not unlike when you buy a new car and suddenly you see that car all over town. In the case of hell, we not only believe it is more prevalent in the Bible than it is, due to it being such an integral part of many people's beliefs, but we even apply it to verses that have nothing to do with it, just because they mention fire or judgment.

Do not be misled. The references to *Gehenna* in the New Testament are not too numerous or complicated for you to process. The word appears just twelve times. Eleven of those times it is Jesus who uses it to denote the place where you'd be sentenced to go by God if you were not granted salvation. He uses it three times in the Gospel of Mark, seven times in Matthew, and once in Luke (it is not mentioned in the Gospel of John). The twelfth use, as you'll see, is not by Jesus and comes in a later book in the New Testament.

In most of these references, Jesus says that being a sinner is grounds for the judgment that would land you in *Gehenna*,

---

1 This will cover the *NRSV, NIV, NKJV, ASV, ESV, HCSB, NASB,* and *ISV* translations.

2 There is one other spot where we see the word "hell" towards the end of the Bible, but this use is not a translation of *Gehenna* and will be addressed later in this chapter.

and he issues these warnings in order to help you live a righteous life and save you from this fate.

In the first verse, we see that you are a sinner if you treat others poorly, and this sin could land you in *Gehenna*:

1) But I say to you that if you are angry with a brother or sister, you will be liable to judgment; and if you insult a brother or sister, you will be liable to the council; and if you say, "You fool," you will be liable to the *Gehenna* of fire. (Matthew 5:22)

In the second verse, which contains the widely quoted biblical description of *Gehenna* as "unquenchable fire," Jesus also warns of the peril of sin:

2) If your hand causes you to stumble,[1] cut it off; it is better for you to enter life[2] maimed than to have two hands and to go to *Gehenna*, to the unquenchable fire. (Mark 9:43)

The important message Jesus relays here is that you must do anything you can to avoid living in sin, because if you are a sinner at the time of your judgment, you'll go to *Gehenna*. He is not talking about going there for not believing in him. The

---

1 Term for sin.
2 Referring to eternal life.

definition of sin here is any action that would keep you from being righteous—from living according to God's will.

If you are beginning to feel uncomfortable, bear in mind that what we are discussing in this chapter has nothing to do with your acceptance of Jesus Christ as your Lord and Savior, nor are we attempting to define God's criteria for salvation or how to get to heaven. What we are addressing is how specific verses from scripture have been improperly co-opted to threaten your soul with hell.

In Matthew and Mark, Jesus uses hyperbole five more times when mentioning sin as the reason for you to end up in *Gehenna* (cut off your hand, your foot, or tear out your eye, depending on which is the cause of your sin).

3) If your right eye causes you to sin, gouge it out and throw it away. It is better for you to lose one part of your body than for your whole body to be thrown into *Gehenna*. (Matthew 5:29)

4) And if your right hand causes you to sin, cut if off and throw it away. It is better for you to lose one part of your body than for your whole body to go into *Gehenna*. (Matthew 5:30)

5) And if your foot causes you to stumble, cut it off; it is better for you to enter life lame than to have two feet and to be thrown into *Gehenna*. (Mark 9:45)

6) And if your eye causes you to stumble, tear it out; it is better for you to enter the kingdom of God with one eye than to have two eyes and to be thrown into *Gehenna,* where their worm never dies, and the fire is never quenched. (Mark 9:47–48)

7) And if your eye causes you to sin, gouge it out and throw it away. It is better for you to enter life with one eye than to have two eyes and be thrown into the fire of *Gehenna.* (Matthew 18:9)

As you can see, more than half the verses in which the word *Gehenna* is used have nothing to do with your belief in Jesus. This should be *very* important, shouldn't it? Jesus himself tells you in these verses that sin is what can cause you to land in *Gehenna.*

The next two examples are parallel verses[1] from the Gospels of Matthew and Luke, and here the main message is for you to fear God, the one who can send you to *Gehenna.* In these verses, Jesus is prepping his disciples to go out and spread his messages. He encourages them to be unafraid if they are not accepted by people or towns, or if they are persecuted by religious authorities, because God is with them. He tells them, in essence, not to fear those who can only hurt them physically but to fear only God.

---

1 A parallel verse is one that is repeated and virtually the same in more than one Gospel, although there may be slight variations.

8) Do not fear those who kill the body but cannot kill the soul; rather fear him who can destroy both soul and body in *Gehenna*. (Matthew 10:28)

9) I tell you my friends, do not fear those who kill the body and after that can do nothing more. But I will warn you whom to fear: fear him who, after he has killed, has authority to cast into *Gehenna*. Yes, I tell you, fear him! (Luke 12:4–5)

In the next two verses, the word *Gehenna* is used in passing to indicate where a group of scribes and Pharisees, whom Jesus is addressing, deserve to go due to their hypocrisy (as you might say figuratively of a politician you don't like, "He'll be going straight to hell."). In these cases, Jesus reproaches the men because they don't do themselves what they preach for others to do, and they claim to be pious but are driven only by their desire to be recognized as religious authorities.

10) Woe to you, scribes and Pharisees, hypocrites! For you cross sea and land to make a single convert, and you make the new convert twice as much a child of *Gehenna* as yourselves. (Matthew 23:15)

11) You snakes, you brood of vipers! How can you escape being sentenced to *Gehenna?* (Matthew 23:33)

Jesus certainly gets into heated exchanges at times with scribes and Pharisees, and he might be declaring they will go to *Gehenna* because of who they are (other variations of sinners), but the verses are not saying they (or you) will go there for not believing in his divinity.

The last of our twelve examples is the only time the word *Gehenna* is used in the New Testament and it is not Jesus who says it. It appears in the Epistle of James (one of the books in the latter part of the New Testament). This verse mentions *Gehenna* to make a point, similar to the previous two examples, but its main subject is how the tongue leads us to sin.

12) The tongue also is a fire, a world of evil among the parts of the body. It corrupts the whole body, sets the whole course of one's life on fire, and is itself set on fire by *Gehenna*. (James 3:6)

As you can see, none of the twelve verses containing the word *Gehenna* use it as a consequence or threat for you not believing in Jesus as the Lord. The doctrine of fear has been ever based on an unwritten assumption of what the Bible says, which many of us were taught growing up, and throughout our lives.

The Rich Man and Lazarus

There is a story in the Gospel of Luke, *The Rich Man and Lazarus,* which warrants a lengthier examination here, because to this day, countless people have taken the story to be referring to hell.[1] As you'll see, however, the fiery place it mentions is not at all the same place as *Gehenna*. It is an easy misconception to make because the story sure seems to be describing our idea of hell, however, the place mentioned in it is Hades, a term from Greek mythology, which is not the same as what we generally believe in as hell. In addition, you'll see that Jesus did not intend for the story to be taken literally.

Jesus tells us there was a rich man who ate sumptuously every day. Lazarus, a poor and starving man, would camp out at his door, hoping to get any scraps of food that fell from the man's table. Both men died, and Lazarus was carried away by angels to be with Abraham, while the rich man went to Hades—a place where he was tormented by flames. The rich man begged Abraham to let Lazarus come and cool his tongue with some drops of cool water, but Abraham reminded the rich man that in life he had received good things while Lazarus had received evil, and now, in death, those roles were reversed.

All the other times we see the English word hell in the Gospels it is a translation of the Greek word *Gehenna*. In the past, for many centuries, the word Hades in Luke's story was mistranslated as "hell," but has long since been corrected.[2]

The Hades of Greek mythology is a term that refers to the underworld (named after Hades, the god of the underworld). But whereas our concept of hell was probably influenced by the concept of Hades, our religious beliefs are very different

---

1 Luke 16:19–31.

2 The *NRSV* and *NIV* Bibles correctly use the word Hades in this passage from Luke. Only the old *KJV (King James Version)* Bible used the word hell. The *New King James Version* has since updated their text and uses Hades as well.

from those of the ancient Greeks. For example, in Greek mythology, the god Hades was not viewed as evil; he was simply the overseer of the underworld, which is very different from the way many of us view Satan, the overseer of hell, as the personification of evil. In addition, Hades was a place where *all* souls went after death, not just the wicked. In this story in Luke, however, Hades is used as a place where the wicked go.

With the history and influence of the Greek culture in the Mediterranean region, Hades would have been a common reference for those who lived there. With *The Rich Man and Lazarus,* Jesus is telling us a story, rather than speaking directly, and he uses Hades as a literary device to tell us there is judgment and punishment for not being righteous. This is very different from the specific admonishments you read earlier in which he tells us to avoid sin so that we don't end up in the actual valley of *Gehenna* outside Jerusalem.

To Jesus, *Gehenna* is an actual place—biblical nonfiction; Hades is a place in mythology—biblical fiction. It's comparable to someone telling you about a trip they took to New York City where they visited the Empire State Building, versus your reading a novel in which the character visits the Empire State building. In the Gospels, this is a distinction of major importance because our hell and Hades are not the same thing—one is real and one is not—they both refer to a place of fiery punishment but that is all they have in common.

The main point of Jesus' Lazarus story is not to tell us there is a hell, but to indicate that people should be righteous, because who we are has consequences, for better or worse. In this case, if you are rich, you should share what you have and give to the poor.

We also know Jesus was telling us a story, rather than speaking about an actual hell, by looking at the context of where *The Rich Man and Lazarus* appears in the Gospel of Luke. It is the sixth in a series of parables told in Luke and, therefore, like those preceding it, was not meant to be taken literally. A parable, by definition, is a story that conveys a lesson or truth beyond the literal meaning of the words. Jesus often taught through parables in Matthew, Mark, and Luke.

The first of the two parables preceding the Lazarus story begins, "There was a man who had two sons..."[1] This is the parable of the return of the prodigal son, who asked his father to give him his inheritance early, which the son then squandered entirely in wild living, ended up broke and starving, and then came back to beg for his father's help. Rather than chastise him or cast him out, his father embraced and kissed him. "The Son said, 'Father, I have sinned against heaven and against you. I am no longer worthy to be called your son.' But the father said to his servants, 'Let's have a feast and celebrate. For this son of mine was dead and is alive again; he was lost and is found.'"[2]

This is a story specifically intended to teach the lesson that no matter how bad you've been, even though you are "dead," you can come back to life—be lost and then found—ever loved by your Father in heaven.

The next parable begins, "There was a rich man who had

1 Luke 15:11.
2 Luke 15:21–24.

a manager..."[1] This is another invented story used to convey a message. Then the story of Lazarus begins, "There was a rich man who was dressed in purple..." We therefore know right away, from how Jesus begins the story, that it, too, is a parable, and his use of a fiery place was not intended literally.

This leaves us only to address a thirteenth and last time we see the word hell in our English translations of the New Testament. It appears in 2 Peter, which is found near the end of the New Testament, and is very different from the other twelve times we see the word hell. In this instance, "hell" is not a translation of *Gehenna*, but of *Tartarus*, another term from Greek mythology that originally referred to the lowest region of the underworld (named after the deity *Tartarus*).

But it is clear just from the context here that this hell is nothing like *Gehenna* of the Gospels. In fact, *Tartarus* is not even used here to indicate a place where humans were sent; it is where God sent angels who have sinned.

> For if God did not spare the angels when they
> sinned, but cast them into *Tartarus* and committed
> them to chains of deepest darkness to be kept until
> the judgment; (2 Peter 2:4)

---

1 Luke 16:1.

We have now covered all the instances in which we see the word hell in our English New Testaments, but there are other verses where the word is not used that we have nevertheless interpreted to refer to our idea of hell, which we must look at next.

CHAPTER 7

ETERNAL FIRE

Aside from the twelve verses in which the word *Gehenna* is used, there are other verses where Jesus refers to a judgment resulting in fire. In the Gospel of Mark, for example, he mentions a place where "the fire is never quenched."[1] Or, in the verse below from the Gospel of Matthew, which is much the same as those you've already read, he uses "eternal fire" instead of *Gehenna*.

> If your hand or foot causes you to sin, cut it off and throw it away. It is better for you to enter life maimed or crippled than to have two hands or two feet and be thrown into eternal fire. (Matthew 18:8)

Another one of these references to eternal fire is also found in Matthew, where Jesus says:

---

1 Mark 9:48.

You that are accursed, depart from me into the
eternal fire prepared for the devil and his angels.
(Matthew 25:41)

This is one of the sources for the imagery of "eternal fire"
that permeates our culture. I've often heard this verse quoted
in sermons to show us there is a hell in the Bible. But we need
to ask, who are the "accursed" being referred to in that verse?
It can seem like the accursed were those who didn't believe in
Jesus, because that is typically what we're told is the criterion
for one's going to hell.

But like the verses you read in the last chapter in which
Jesus says you'd be thrown into *Gehenna* for being a sinner,
the reasons he gives here for your being accursed and possibly ending up in the eternal fire are based on who you were—
what you did and how you treated others—not on your belief
in him.

This particular section of Matthew exemplifies some of
the most important and powerful messages Jesus gave us concerning judgment.

When determining the meaning of scriptural verses, the
surrounding verses often provide context that is essential for
understanding. In the above quote from Matthew, Jesus is
talking about a time when a figure called the Son of Man will
come to earth to judge all people. The Gospel wants us to
know that the Son of Man referred to here is Jesus and he will
be the one returning to judge, because in the next chapter of

Matthew, Jesus says, "the Son of Man will be handed over to be crucified."[1]

To paraphrase from Matthew, Jesus says that when the Son comes, he will sit on his throne as king and gather all the nations before him. Then he will separate them as a shepherd would separate his sheep from his goats. He will put the sheep on his right hand and the goats on his left. He will tell those on his right that they are blessed by God and will inherit the kingdom of heaven:[2]

> 'For I was hungry and you gave me food, I was
> thirsty and you gave me something to drink, I was
> a stranger and you welcomed me, I was naked and
> you gave me clothing, I was sick and you took care
> of me, I was in prison and you visited me.' Then
> the righteous will answer him, 'Lord, when was it
> that we gave you food, or something to drink, or
> welcomed you, or gave you clothing, or saw you
> sick or in prison and visited you?'[3] And the king
> will answer them, 'Truly I tell you, just as you did it
> to one of the least of these who are members of my
> family, you did it to me.'
>
> Then he will say to those at his left hand, 'You
> that are accursed, depart from me into the eternal

---

1 Matthew 26:2. (The Son of Man and the Son of God are both titles used for Jesus in the Gospels.)

2 Matthew 25:31–34.

3 Verse abridged.

fire prepared for the devil and his angels; for I was hungry and you gave me no food, I was thirsty and you gave me nothing to drink, I was a stranger and you did not welcome me, naked and you did not give me clothing, sick and in prison and you did not visit me.' Then they will also answer, 'Lord, when was it that we saw you hungry or thirsty or a stranger or naked or sick or in prison, and did not take care of you?' Then he will answer them, 'Truly I tell you, just as you did not do it to one of the least of these, you did not do it to me.' And these will go away into eternal punishment, but the righteous into eternal life. (Matthew 25:35–46)

Jesus is saying in these verses that those who turned their backs on their fellow human beings in need were also, implicitly, turning their backs on him. The righteous, who helped their fellow human beings in need, were also helping him.

In fact, neither the righteous sheep nor the accursed goats had ever seen or known Jesus. They ask him plainly, "Lord, when was it that we saw you?" and Jesus explains that how they treated other people is how they treated him. The fact that they've never seen him (or believed in him) is irrelevant. The only issue is whether they were righteous or wicked.

He speaks elsewhere in Matthew about judgment's being determined by one's righteousness or lack thereof. Here are a couple of other examples:

Not everyone who says to me, 'Lord Lord,' will
enter the kingdom of heaven, but only the one
who does the will of my Father in heaven.
(Matthew 7:21)

For I tell you, unless your righteousness exceeds
that of the scribes and Pharisees, you will never
enter the kingdom of heaven. (Matthew 5:20)

One of the most frightening (and popular) images of hell
comes from the Book of Revelation:

And the devil who had deceived them was thrown
into the lake of fire and brimstone,[1] where the
beast and the false prophet were, and they will be
tormented day and night forever and ever.
(Revelation 20:10)

Here you are presented with another eternal fire, this time
in the image of a lake of fire. All of these fiery depictions have
fueled our darkest imaginings for many centuries following

---

1 Most modern Bibles translate this as "fire and sulfur." "Fire and
brimstone" comes from the King James Bible, and I use it because it
seems to me still the more familiar term in our culture.

their being written, right up and into the present day. While the verse speaks of what will happen to the devil, Revelation then goes on to say what could cause you to go there as well:

...and anyone whose name was not found written in the book of life was thrown into the lake of fire. (Revelation 20:15)

The "book of life" is a term from the Old Testament. It refers to the book in which God lists the names of the righteous. The basis for his judgment is clarified in a previous verse from Revelation:

...Also another book was opened, the book of life. And the dead were judged according to their works, as recorded in the books. (Revelation 20:12)

According to what it says here, you will be judged according to your actions—what you have done (your works), not by whether or not you believe in Jesus.

As a reminder, nothing said here is intended to make a case for how God determines if you will be saved on the day of judgment. This is about hell—showing case-by-case how specific verses have been improperly annexed to threaten you with hell.

The Timing of Judgment

Up until now, we've mostly addressed the believe part of the believe-or-burn doctrine—the criteria for deciding whether or not you could end up in God's eternal fire. Now for the burn part. If you accept that Jesus was referring to an actual eternal fire, or an actual place *Gehenna,* which we translated and accepted as our hell, a crucial and hugely underrated question must be asked: When would this hellfire you've been threatened with occur? Perhaps the answer seems obvious: after you die. But if you read what Jesus had to say about it in the Gospels, you will find that this place of God's fire, where you could be sent after you die, is nowhere to be found.

The passage from Matthew about the sheep and the goats speaks about a time when the Son of Man, Jesus, will come from the heavens to judge all people. The time Jesus is referring to in that passage does not pertain to a place you could go to after your particular life naturally ends. Rather, it refers to the occasion of God's final judgment of humanity, which will end the world as we know it—aka, the day of judgment; or, the apocalypse.

"When the Son of Man comes in his glory, and all the angels with him, then he will sit on the throne of his glory."[1] At that time, Jesus will usher in a new age, sometimes called the kingdom of heaven,[2] which is when the sheep (the righteous) will be blessed by God and inherit eternal life in the kingdom of heaven, while the accursed goats (the wicked) will go to the eternal fire. Jesus preaches about the coming of judgment

---

1 Matthew 25:30, similarly said in Mark 13:26 and Luke 21:27.
2 Mark and Luke call it the kingdom of God.

day throughout Matthew, Mark, and Luke (though Luke also begins to transition away from it), and it is the over-arching context for all eleven times Jesus uses the word *Gehenna*, as well as the context for all his references to the punishment of fire for the wicked.

He further tells us that the Son of Man comes to judge all of humanity—not just the living but all the dead will also be resurrected to face judgment—he will fulfill a prophecy to that effect from the Old Testament.[1] Jesus will end the world as we know it and transform it into a new world—the kingdom of heaven on earth—earth restored to an Eden-like place, and he will rule on the throne of this world forever more.

On the outskirts of the kingdom, in the valley of *Gehenna,* the evildoers and sinners will be thrown into God's fire, but the righteous will inherit the kingdom in which there will be no more death, disease, pain, suffering, sin, and, of course, no more evildoers (sometimes the threat is just *Gehenna* with no fire mentioned, other times the threat is fire with no *Gehenna* mentioned, and a few times Jesus says they will be "thrown into the outer darkness"[2]).

If we want to take his words literally, which we are doing if we say there is a real fire to be thrown into, Jesus did not preach about that happening in an afterlife, only at the end of the world as we know it (hence the expression you are probably familiar with, "the end-times").

---

1 "Everyone whose name is found written in the book will be delivered. Multitudes who sleep in the dust of the earth will awake: some to everlasting life, others to shame and everlasting contempt" (Daniel 12:1–2).

2 Matthew 8:12, 22:13, 25:30.

Similarly, the entire book of Revelation has traditionally been understood to refer to this prophesied time of judgment and has nothing to do with your own personal afterlife. The word "revelation" is derived from the Greek word for apocalypse *(apokalypsis),* which means a "revealing." The author has visions in which God reveals to him all that is imminently happening in the final judgment, whose events have been set in motion with the death of Jesus Christ.

Revelation corroborates that, after the judgment is done, the kingdom of God will be on earth:

> Then the seventh angel blew his trumpet, and there were loud voices in heaven, saying, "The kingdom *of the world* has become the kingdom of our Lord and of his Messiah and he will reign forever and ever." (Revelation 11:15, emphasis added)

> And I heard a loud voice from the throne saying, "See, *the home of God is among mortals.* He will *dwell with them;* they will be his peoples, and God himself will be with them; he will wipe every tear from their eyes. Death will be no more; mourning and crying and pain will be no more, for the first things have passed away."[3]
> (Revelation 21:3–4, emphases added)

---

3 The "first things" refers to the present earth, heaven, and life as we know it, which will be replaced by a new heaven on earth.

The passages show that if you are righteous at the time of judgment you will be made immortal—given eternal life. Jesus tells us in Matthew that at that time, "the righteous will shine like the sun in the kingdom of their Father."[1]

As you can see from the many verses cited in this chapter so far, *Gehenna* and the eternal fires, which Jesus speaks of in the Gospels of Mark, Matthew, and Luke, do not refer to an afterlife place in another dimension where bodiless souls will go depending on how they were judged. It is a place on earth involving real, physical bodies. The judgment is not at the time when one dies a personal death.

Now don't be alarmed. Jesus did speak about his followers having an afterlife in heaven. He mentions it only twice, but it is definitively stated. We see it in one verse in the Gospel of Luke, and there is a more lengthy passage about it in the Gospel of John.

In all four Gospels, heaven is mentioned many times (usually where God resides or where Jesus came from), it's just that Jesus doesn't actually speak about us going there when we die except for the two spots, and the mention of it in Luke barely tells us anything. It comes at the end of his Gospel, when Jesus is on the cross and with two criminals being crucified. One of the criminals mocks him, but the other rebukes that criminal and acknowledges the divine identity of Jesus by saying, "'Jesus, remember me when you come into your kingdom.' Jesus answered him, 'Today you will be with me in Paradise.'"[2] But that is all Jesus tells us there about heaven.

---

1 Matthew 13:43.
2 Luke 23:43.

The reference to an afterlife heaven in the Gospel of John is much more important, and will be discussed in a later chapter devoted to salvation.

Matthew's References to a Fiery Judgment

Have you ever had the experience of hearing an old-school Sunday sermon about what it will be like on judgment day? You might have heard biblical verses cited quickly as you flipped through the pages to keep up with the preacher (if you were so inclined). In a series of quick glances, you saw menacing eternal fires, people being thrown into burning furnaces, weeping and the gnashing of teeth. All that, plus the preacher's message about how to avoid these terrifying things, no doubt got into your head. The sermon ended, you closed the book and went on your way. But all the while those images played upon your subconscious as you went about your daily life. Such talk might seem outdated to some, though it is alive and still current to many others. Regardless, this material comes from the Bible, and so it remains underlying many people's beliefs.

Almost all the references to the day of judgment that involve terrifying graphic imagery of your being thrown into fire (that don't specifically mention *Gehenna*), appear in Matthew. In Matthew, chapter 3, John the Baptist is blasting the Pharisees with his warning of the "wrath to come,"[3] threatening that "every tree therefore that does not bear good fruit is cut down and thrown into the fire."[4] There is no question about

---

3 Matthew 3:7; also in Luke 3:7.
4 Matthew 3:10; Jesus says this also in Matthew 7:19 and Luke 3:9.

what he means. The "wrath to come" is a common biblical reference to the final judgment (along with "day of wrath" or sometimes "God's wrath").[1] And with the wrath comes the fire.

Two verses later, he delivers this message another way when he refers to the proverbial separation of the wheat from the chaff: "He [Jesus] will gather his wheat into the granary; but the chaff he will burn with unquenchable fire."[2]

Then, later in Matthew, Jesus states definitively:

> The kingdom of heaven may be compared to someone who sowed good seed in his field; ... at harvest time I will tell the reapers, "Collect the weeds first and bind them in bundles to be burned, but gather the wheat into my barn." (Matthew 13:24, 30)

We don't have to speculate about what Jesus means there, because a few verses later he explains the parable to his disciples, who did not understand it:

> The one who sows the good seed is the Son of Man; the field is the world, and the good seed are the children of the kingdom; the weeds are the children of the evil one, and the enemy who sowed them is the devil; *the harvest is the end of the age,* and the

---

1 Job 21:30; Proverbs 11:4; Isaiah 13:9; Psalm 110:5; Romans 2:5; Revelation 6:17... to name just a few places the term appears.
2 Matthew 3:12; also in Luke 3:17.

reapers are angels. Just as the weeds are collected
and burned up with fire, so will it be *at the end of
the age.* (Matthew 13:37–40, emphases added)

The wheat and the weeds (or the chaff) are the people
who do God's will and the people who do the evil one's will,
respectively, and they will be separated accordingly at the
time of the final judgment—similar meaning as the sheep and
the goats, just a different metaphor.

The same message about judgment day is repeated twice
more and even more explicitly in the following verses:

The Son of Man will send his angels, and they
will collect out of his kingdom all causes of sin
and all evildoers, and they will throw them into
the furnace of fire, where there will be weeping
and gnashing of the teeth. (Matthew 13:41–42)

So it will be *at the end of the age.* The angels will
come out and separate the evil from the righteous
and throw them into the furnace of fire, where
there will be weeping and gnashing of the teeth.
(Matthew 13:49–50, emphasis added)

As the final example here, from the Gospel of Luke, Jesus
again speaks of the time when the Son of Man will come to
render God's final judgment:

But on the day that Lot left Sodom, it rained
fire and sulfur from heaven and destroyed all
of them—it will be like that on the day that the Son
of Man is revealed. (Luke 17:29–30)

Note that none of these examples say anything to indicate there is an afterlife hell where you could go to—not the
slightest crumb to nourish that idea. There are, however, specific, incontrovertible references to the end of this world as we
know it (this age), when the Son of Man comes, and at that
time it will be the righteous and evildoers who are separated,
not the believers and nonbelievers. In several places it says
that the evildoers will be thrown into the fire—be it the fire of
Gehenna, the furnace of fire, or the eternal fire—they're going
into God's fire. And, as you will see in the next chapter, even
those thrown into the fire will not suffer for an eternity—even
then they are not being thrown into what people call hell.

If rather than "believe or burn," you believe that only if
you're an evildoer will you burn, the same biblical truths apply. If you believe that the place *Gehenna,* or any of the other
mentions of a fiery judgment, are actually referring to a real
hell, there are simply no words at all saying you could be sent
there when you die.

If you have any doubts about the timing of when evildoers
will be judged, you can check your Bible and see for yourself. If you read the scripture objectively, these truths will be
self-evident, and you will be surprised that you never noticed
before exactly what the verses were saying. It will be as if you

had walked down a street a hundred times and never noticed a giant tree that had always been there.

So what about all the other references Jesus made to *Gehenna* or other forms of eternal fire? There aren't any. We've covered them all. The threat of hell has been grossly overstated and misrepresented. The examples in this chapter and the one prior are the recycled fuel that has kept the fire raging for all these many centuries, and you can still feel the heat on your face today.

What the Bible actually teaches can greatly conflict with our commonly held beliefs about hell, and coming to understand that can initially be very disconcerting. None of this has anything to do with one's faith in Jesus or God. But for anyone who believes that the Bible is the Word of God, the foundation upon which our faith rests, shouldn't we know exactly what is written there, and make sure our beliefs are supported by it? Even if we say our foundation is faith in Jesus, not the Bible, the fact is that everything we know or believe of what he said and did comes from the Bible.

There would be no reason for any of us to question what we know about hell unless we were inclined to study scripture and research it on our own. If we were taught something growing up and throughout our lives, and if we trust the source of that information, it's only natural that we would accept what we were told and not think to examine it.

The question is, what do we do when we receive new

WHAT THE HELL IS HELL?

information that conflicts with something we believe to be true? The immediate reaction of our ego might be to dismiss it instantly, in order to protect our status quo. Our ego doesn't want confusion, uncertainty, or doubt; it doesn't want us to be vulnerable. As we discussed in earlier chapters, however, it is actually protecting itself, because if we have any cause for self-examination, or to do some *soul*-searching, we might discover exactly what the ego is doing and realize we don't want to live under its domination.

Our ego will therefore strongly deflect such examination, claiming that whatever conflicts with what we believe to be true is simply dead wrong—no further action required. Perhaps it even goes a step further by telling us that our faith is being tested. The ego can be diabolically clever.

If we decide to take up the challenge that the new information might present to our beliefs, the first step we must take is to do the research to see if what we've been told is true or false. If we find that the new information is false, we can be reinforced in our beliefs because we have learned the truth for ourselves. If we find that the new information is correct, and it is only new because we haven't been made aware of it before, we must ask ourselves: Would God ever expect us to turn away from the truth? God is truth, wouldn't you agree? So why would we ever have to fear the truth?

If we are to answer the question, "What is hell?" and if we believe the Bible is to be taken literally, we must begin by becoming aware of the fact that, in our English Bibles, whenever Jesus uses the word hell or refers to fiery judgment, he does so entirely in the context of the day of judgment. If the language is not to be taken literally, we might be having a very different conversation, discussing, for example, whether hellfire and furnaces of fire were actually intended as graphic metaphors for the consequences of sin or unrighteousness. But, so long as we continue to believe that hell is a real place to which we could go when we die, we can't then turn around and take the position that it is metaphorical when mentioned in the Bible.[1]

⚜

We have now discussed all the places in the Bible where Jesus talks about *Gehenna* and fire you could be thrown into. We've talked about *why*, according to Jesus, you'd go to *Gehenna* (for being a sinner or unrighteous/wicked). We've talked about *when* you'd go there (the day of judgment). So what exactly is *Gehenna*, anyway? We've discussed the basics about it, but in order to understand what that word meant to Jesus, we need to know more about it, and delve deeper into what final judgment of the wicked meant to him.

---

1 62% of Americans believe in a literal hell "where people...experience physical suffering, and are prevented from having a relationship with God," according to: "Views on the afterlife," Pew Research Center, Washington, D.C. https://www.pewforum.org/2021/11/23/views-on-the-afterlife/

CHAPTER 8

DID JESUS PREACH ABOUT ETERNAL TORMENT?

In order to answer that question according to the Bible and not our beliefs, we need to go back to the Old Testament, which is where *Gehenna* of the New Testament originated.

As you read earlier, the valley of *Gehenna* came to be known as an abominable, desecrated place where children were sacrificed by fire in cultic worship of the pagan god Molech. The valley was, and still is, a real place on earth outside Jerusalem. There could be a whole chapter discussing the several mentions of the valley in the Old Testament, but I will give just two crucially important excerpts to help show how Jesus understood and used the term *Gehenna*.

The first excerpt, from the book of Jeremiah the prophet, tells us most of what we need to know concerning the valley. (Reminder: in the Old Testament it is referred to as the valley of Hinnom, or of the son of Hinnom, which is a translation of the Hebrew *Ge-Hinnom*):

For the people of Judah[1] have done evil in my sight, says the Lord; they have set their abominations in the house that is called my name, defiling it. And they go on building the high place of Topeth, which is in the valley of the son of Hinnom, to burn their sons and their daughters in the fire—which I did not command, nor did it come to my mind. Therefore, the days are surely coming, says the Lord, when it will no more be called Topeth or the valley of the son of Hinnom, but the valley of Slaughter: for they will bury in Topeth until there is no more room. The corpses of this people will be food for the birds of the air, and for the animals of the earth; and no one will frighten them away. (Jeremiah 7:30–33)

As you can see, *Gehenna* is the place where the Lord will take out his wrath upon the wicked, whom he deems here to be those people of Judah. Notice that the fire is associated with the child sacrifice at *Gehenna*; the verses do not, however, say that God will exact *his* judgment though fire. He will slaughter, which is typically executed with a sword or blade. All that will be left is the corpses for the birds and animals to feed on—not even the corpses will be burned—they will be buried.

Remember, this *Gehenna* is what we came to translate as our "hell," and we can already see again how different the actual *Gehenna* of the Bible is from our idea of hell. This is a real place with real things happening.

---

1 Around 930 BC the kingdom of Israel was split; the southern half was named Judah; the northern half retained the name Israel.

God does, however, use fire to execute his judgment else-where in the Old Testament, which led to its use as a method of punishment in the New Testament. In the book of Isaiah, the prophet speaks about a time when the nation of Judah was overthrown by the Babylonians, which eventually led to a major number of Judeans being exiled.

In Isaiah chapters 56–66, the Judeans are finally returning home from exile, but times are tough and the people once again resort to pagan practices, such as child sacrifice, thinking it will help them. That is among the transgressions of the wicked in the nation for which God will exact judgment.

> For the Lord will come in fire, and his chariots like the whirlwind, to pay back his anger in fury [to the wicked], and his rebuke in flames of fire. For by fire will the Lord execute judgment, and by his sword, on all flesh; and those slain by the Lord shall be many. (Isaiah 66:15–16)

The second verse, below, is essential to know because we see it quoted in the Gospel of Mark. The Lord says:

> And they [the righteous] shall go out and look at the dead bodies of the people who have rebelled against me; for their worm shall not die, their fire shall not be quenched, and they shall be an abhorrence to all flesh. (Isaiah 66:24)

Notice something easy to overlook in these verses: the unquenchable fire is not how God will execute his judgment—that comes from his chariot with flames and sword to slay all, as shown in the prior verses. The unquenchable fire comes *later,* to deal with all the corpses. Also, in Isaiah, the righteous are seeing the dead bodies of the wicked being burned up in the fire. This is all happening in the world.

What is also important to keep in mind as we go forward here is that neither Jeremiah nor Isaiah was talking about the day of judgment that Jesus talks about in the Gospels. Both prophets were talking about the Lord's judging a localized region or peoples for their transgressions and destroying them—in both of these cases it is people in the Israelite nation of Judah—not the whole world.

The unquenchable fire in Isaiah then got carried forward into the Gospel of Mark. Jesus says, "And if your eye causes you to stumble, tear it out; it is better for you to enter the kingdom of God with one eye than to have two eyes and to be thrown into *Gehenna*, 'where their worm never dies, and the fire is never quenched'"[1] (that last part quotes Isaiah). And a few verses prior to that he says, "it is better for you to enter life maimed than to have two hands and to go to *Gehenna*, to the unquenchable fire."[2] Matthew and Luke also equate judgment of the wicked with "unquenchable fire" in their Gospels.[3] The borrowed imagery is showing us that they will be thrown into the valley of *Gehenna,* into the real fire there.

---

1 Mark 9:47–48, which quotes Isaiah 66:24.
2 Mark 9:43.
3 Matthew 3:12; Luke 3:17.

Perhaps Jesus chose this site of *Gehenna* as ground zero for the fire where the wicked will be thrown into on the day of judgment because of it being an abominable, cursed place. Whatever the case may be, Jesus knew his own scripture. He would have known exactly what *Gehenna* was, and what Isaiah's unquenchable fire was—a fire to dispose of all the bodies God had slain. He would have known that the corpses burning in that fire would be in the same place on earth within the view of the righteous.

In what version of our heaven and hell can the righteous in heaven see bodies burning in hell?

These references from the Old Testament follow the narrative of a judgment to come on earth. This gives us the final corroborating evidence that *Gehenna* is not the afterlife hell with which we are familiar—*and what an important thing to know that is.*

In the decades and centuries after Jesus died, however, our imaginations added something else the Bible does not say: that anyone sent to *Gehenna* would suffer in the fire for all eternity.

The Fate of the Wicked

Looking back on the verses already cited, you will see that Jesus spoke of the wicked as being *destroyed* in the fire, not burning forever. He specifically uses the term "destroyed" three times in verses where he mentions the final judgment, and in several other places he refers to the destruction in other ways.

> Do not fear those who kill the body but cannot kill the
> soul; rather fear him who can *destroy* both soul and
> body in *Gehenna*. (Matthew 10:28, emphasis added)

In what version of our hell are souls destroyed? If our soul
were destroyed, how could we suffer for all eternity? And what
hell have we heard of that has *physical bodies* thrown into it?
As we've seen in many cases now, it's easy to be unaware of
the actual language used because we believe what we've been
taught and never had cause to look into it ourselves.

> They were eating and drinking, and marrying and being
> given in marriage, until the day Noah entered the ark,
> and the flood came and *destroyed* all of them. Likewise,
> just as it was in the days of Lot: they were eating and
> drinking, buying and selling, planting and building,
> but on the day that Lot left Sodom, it rained fire and
> sulfur from heaven and *destroyed* all of them—it will
> be like *that* on the day that the Son of Man is revealed.
> (Luke 17:27–30, emphases added)

Jesus draws upon the same concept of destruction as we
saw in the passages from Jeremiah and Isaiah. God is going to
destroy the people who did evil; not sentence them to eternal
torment. In the passage above, the fire and sulfur destroys the
wicked, it is not what God throws people into alive where

they suffer for eternity. Our common idea that hell *is* the unquenchable or eternal fire is not biblically supported.

Now, the word destruction might have a metaphorical meaning. In modern terms, one basketball fan might say to another, "Our team is going to destroy yours." The only way for that to work, however, is to interpret the entire context of the verses as metaphor—fire and all (and perhaps we would be wise to view scripture in non-literal terms more often than we do). But we can at least say that the most common definition of the term "destroy" (to put an end to; kill; annihilate), as stated in scripture, seems to have been overlooked by a great many of us. Here, however, we are concerned with what the Bible actually says, versus the belief taught for ages that we will suffer for all eternity if we are sentenced to hell on the day of judgment.

Jesus repeats what he means by destruction a few different ways: "at harvest time I will tell the reapers, 'Collect the weeds first and bind them in bundles to be burned, but gather the wheat into my barn.'"[1] In modern terms, let's say you have a fire going in your backyard and you pull up the weeds and throw them into the flames. What happens? They burn up and are destroyed; they don't burn forever. When Jesus goes on to explain these metaphors to his disciples, he says, "the weeds are the children of the evil one ... the reapers are angels ... and just as the weeds are collected and burned up with fire, so will it be at the end of the age."[2]

The wicked will be burnt up in fire—to exist no more; forever separated from God by virtue of being destroyed.

1 Matthew 13:30.
2 Matthew 13:38–40.

They will not continue to exist, burning in gruesome agony in eternal fire while simultaneously suffering the misery of being aware that they are permanently separated from God. That idea came long after the Gospels were written. You will not find it in the Bible.

Jesus goes on to repeat this message twice more in the Gospel of Matthew, when he says, "evildoers will be thrown into the furnace of fire."[1] In these two verses he also adds, "where there will be weeping and gnashing of the teeth," but that's the most he has to say about what suffering will be experienced in that fire. Based on the fact that Jesus quotes Isaiah in the Gospels, and Isaiah told us that the suffering of the unrighteous would be in view of the righteous, it's a good deduction that the imagery Jesus uses is to convey that the unrighteous will be weeping and gnashing their teeth in envy and despair as they gaze for the last time on the righteous in the kingdom of heaven on earth, or at least in realizing they won't be there.

All these examples are different ways of saying, as Jesus did in Luke, that just as the wicked were destroyed at Sodom, so will they be at the end of the age on the day of judgment.

⚜⚜⚜⚜⚜

There is one instance in the sheep and goats verses you read (pg. 102) where Jesus says that the accursed who did not care for their fellow human beings will go to "eternal punishment." Throughout the ages and to this day, that has

---

1 Matthew 13:41–42, 49–50.

been believed to mean a perpetually felt physical suffering in the afterlife hell, lasting for all eternity. But that belief contradicts the fact that the evildoers will be destroyed by God, which is what the Bible says. Which is right—our belief or the Bible? They can't both be right.

However, consider that punishment could simply mean the very same destruction. At the final judgment, when all the righteous are given eternal life in the kingdom of God, the wicked will be only destroyed. Their eternal punishment is they will be forever outside the kingdom, because they forever do not exist, leaving them in a state of shame and everlasting contempt. Because the wicked were raised from the dead and destroyed, they can never undo their wickedness, and thus the contempt of their wickedness is everlasting (the revulsion of it), not their suffering.[2]

In fact, and to really put closure to all this, the Book of Revelation even goes on to prophesy that after all the dead people have been raised and judged, even death itself will be killed, to exist no more.

> And the sea gave up the dead that were in them, Death and Hades gave up the dead that were in them, and all were judged according to what they had done. Then Death and Hades were thrown into the lake of fire. This is the second death, the lake of fire.
> (Revelation 20:13–14)

---

2 Think of how we will always hold Adolf Hitler in contempt; the contempt is everlasting.

The last words of this verse are hugely important. When people naturally die it is their first death. At the final judgment, however, when all the dead are raised, the evildoers endure their second and final death, as they are destroyed in the lake of fire. It is different vocabulary and imagery from what we see in Matthew, Mark, and Luke, but the idea is the same. Death here means death; it does not mean everlasting suffering. Remember, in the kingdom of heaven on earth, God has done away with death; the righteous become immortal.

In addition to showing us that death itself will be destroyed on the day of judgment, this passage also puts to rest once and for all that Hades could mean hell. It shows us that even in Luke's parable of *The Rich Man and Lazarus*, where Hades was described as a place where the wicked would go, it was only temporary, and eventually it, along with all the dead wicked people there who will be resurrected on the day of judgment, would be finally destroyed in the lake of fire.

If Hades were meant to have the same meaning as our hell, how does that last quote from Revelation work exactly? Hell is destroyed in the lake of fire that is hell? That makes no sense. Since most of us who believe in a hell believe you suffer there for all eternity, Hades cannot be hell, because Hades gets destroyed. Hell, as we commonly understand it, cannot be destroyed because, if it were, you couldn't suffer for all eternity there. *This, too, is so important to remember,* because Luke's story of Lazarus is often misunderstood as talking about our hell.

In light of everything you've read in the last three chapters, can we now have a reality check based on common sense? Does this brutal, vengeful God and the horrific threat of everlasting suffering really sound reasonable to us in this day and age? These are ancient primitive beliefs that, because they have been linked to God and Jesus, people have continued to believe without question to this day. Think about just how cruel and vindictive God would have to be to not only torture you physically for all eternity but also to keep you aware of the fact that the torture would never end. Is that the God you believe in? Many people would answer, "Yes, because that's what the Word of God tells us," but the last three chapters show that it is not what God says.

However you want to interpret all the passages pertaining to *Gehenna* or eternal fires, what you can be sure of by looking into the scripture for yourself is that the Bible never once says you will be tortured forever in *Gehenna*, in a hell, or anywhere else. Then add that fact to all the evidence you've seen here showing that at the final judgment the wicked will simply be destroyed. If you want to believe you could potentially exist eternally in hellfire when you die, that is your choice. It can be tough to break free from a belief so many of us have been taught and held all our lives, but that belief is not supported by scripture.

<hr />

How many of us have been taught the simple proposition, which was said to have come from God, that we either believe in Jesus and go to heaven, or we don't believe and burn in hell? This is not to say that anyone intended harm to us by continuing this teaching, it has simply been passed down for so many centuries that we just accepted what we were told.

According to this doctrine of fear, a) the Bible tells us there is a hell; b) the Bible tells us Jesus is the Son of God; therefore, c) if you don't believe in Jesus you will go to hell when you die. This last teaching is not supported by the Bible.

There are no verses stating there is a hell you could go to after you die. Nor are there any verses that say you will go to hell for not believing in Jesus.[1] And based on whatever criteria you accept for determining final judgment, whether it is belief in Jesus, being a good person, or both, the Bible says the evildoers will be destroyed in the fire, not that they will suffer torment until the end of time. Any other embellishment was added later. The only other option is that Jesus was speaking in metaphorical terms about all of this, which is probably not the way most believers in God view the Bible.

Your faith in Jesus Christ does not demand that you accept all you've been told about hell. Yet, even with the facts being presented to you here, they can be a lot to take in for the first time. I hope you will not take anyone's word on this matter (including mine), but rather seek the truth for yourself. Let the facts presented here serve as a tool to help you verify the truth more swiftly.

You might believe that scripture dictates our idea of hell, but when you are threatened with warnings of why you could end up there and for how long, just make sure you see for yourself what the scripture actually says on these matters.

---

1 There are verses stating there will be *consequences* for not believing. We'll get to those in the next chapters.

There is a major distinction between what is written in the Bible and the beliefs created from interpretation of what is written. If you can find the time, read the New Testament through to the end of Revelation. Separate what is written from what you've been told is meant. Search for your own answers. The matter of your salvation is worth that.

CHAPTER 9

THE SERMON

Like iron dust to a magnet, I have always felt drawn to spiritual words. Even as a young man I enjoyed going to church. Yet, almost every time I went, some of the things I heard would rub me the wrong way. The sermons usually started out with good words of truth, love, and spiritual wisdom, which were valuable and stayed with me. Inevitably, however, the preacher would circle back to a core message: the reaffirmation of the divinity of Jesus Christ and the ramifications of whether or not we accepted him as our Savior.

We had one main preacher and a couple of others on staff who rotated in on leading the Sunday service, but the sermons never changed much. Aside from the basic heaven or hell framework we all knew, we were also reminded at times that we were sinners (lower, flawed beings, weak to temptation) who, for that reason also, could go to hell when we died. But the good news always followed fast: through the grace of Jesus Christ—the higher being, the Son of God—we could be raised up and saved from that fate.

The clear implication was that our spiritual potential to know God was extremely limited relative to that of Jesus, who shared his Father's omniscience and omnipotence. Based on what I read in the Bible, however, that did not seem congruent with what Jesus taught.

Our church valued a dogmatic adherence to its biblical interpretations—it told us what Jesus' words meant and we needed to believe what we were told. Jesus, by contrast, wanted us to seek understanding for ourselves. His ministry didn't seem to me to be about recognizing our limitations and worshiping him; it seemed to be about recognizing our own potential to build a relationship with God, which we could learn to do through Jesus and his teachings. The disconnect between the dogmatic approach we were taught and walking my own path as a seeker led to my eventually learning that religion and spirituality are not the same thing.

I had long since moved away and stopped going to that church, but at some point I had started recording some of the sermons because I wanted to remember what was being said, in order to delve into their messages on my own. On the day of the sermon you'll see quoted on the next pages, I heard the preacher say some wise and meaningful things, but I also heard the same teachings that had always struck me as incorrect and even harmful. I have transcribed two important excerpts here, because they provide a useful context within which to dig deeper into the doctrine of fear and examine where the Bible actually does link negative consequences to not believing in Jesus Christ.

It wouldn't mean much if this sermon or my preacher were unique and this were only my experience. Over the years I have heard many other preachers at various other churches, as well as on TV or online, and have spoken to enough people about their experiences at church to know that this sermon is quite common. Perhaps you've heard sermons like this too:

> There is nothing complicated about the way to God. The Gospel of Christ is clear, short, and irresistible.
>
> God loves you and wants to have a personal relationship with you forever. He wants you to grow close to him and spend eternity with him in heaven after you die.
>
> But one thing separates us from a relationship with God ... sin. Sin is disobeying God. The Bible says in Romans 3:23 that "all have sinned and fall short of the glory of God." Romans goes on to explain that the punishment for sin is death— separation from God in hell forever.[1]
>
> Matthew 25:41 tells us that hell is an everlasting fire, prepared for the devil and his angels.
>
> No matter how hard we try, we can't save ourselves. We can't earn our way to heaven by being good or going to church.
>
> But don't worry! God loves us so much that he sent his only Son, Jesus, to earth. Jesus lived a

---

1 Although the preacher didn't cite the verse number here, he is referencing Romans 6:23. I didn't want to alter any words he said, even to cite a verse number where he didn't.

perfect, sinless life and then died on the cross to take the punishment for our sins. Three days later, he came back to life and now he lives in heaven.

To reach God and live in heaven after you die, you must accept Jesus as your personal Lord and Savior.

Jesus also tells us in Matthew that, "Whoever acknowledges me before other people, I also will acknowledge before my Father in heaven. But whoever disowns me before other people—this could be actually denying him out loud in front of others, or in action caring about the things of this world more than serving the Lord—whoever disowns me, I will disown him to my Father in heaven."[1] Jesus is telling us that to deny him and not have him in the forefront of our lives is a capital sin as concerns our salvation.

This is testified to again by John 15:6, which says, "If a man does not abide in me he is thrown into the fire."

Folks, this fate is easily avoided. To accept Jesus as your Savior, simply talk to God and admit that you are a sinner, believe that Jesus died for your sins and was raised from the dead, and give him control of your life.

---

1 Matthew 10:32–33. When typing this footnote, I realized how impressed we all were and how powerful it was when my preacher, on a roll, quoted verses from memory, often citing the chapter and verse number. This contributed greatly to our trust in him as an authority of scripture and God's messages.

If you accepted Jesus Christ as your Savior, then you can be sure he heard you. Anyone who calls on the name of the Lord will be saved.[2] You have just begun a relationship with God and you will definitely spend eternity in heaven with him.

As we move on to analyzing these two excerpts, I want to point out that it would be easy for both me as the writer and you as the reader to fall into the trap of judging the person delivering the sermon and defining him solely based on whether or not we agree with what he said. The problem is that people are rarely simple to understand or classify as they might seem, which is perhaps part of the reason Jesus advised us not to judge others.[3]

This preacher was a good and loving man who wanted to serve God and his congregation. As I talk about him now, my words are intended only to analyze, as objectively as I can, the words he spoke. It's ironic that what troubled me in sermons like this ultimately inspired and drove me in my lifelong quest for knowledge.

---

2 This is from Romans 10:13.

3 "Do not judge, so that you may not be judged." (Matthew 7:1; Luke 6:37)

The preacher starts off by saying that God wants to have a relationship with us. He ends by saying that we have just begun one (by calling on the name of the Lord). He does guide us into a relationship with God; however, he makes it clear that the closest to God it is possible for us to get while we are on earth is to know that God is up there in heaven. The predominant theme of his sermon is what happens after we die—as if the whole point of our lives on earth is to prepare our souls for death.

What's more, he says we cannot get to heaven to be with God just by being good here on earth, even though that statement directly contradicts Jesus' having said in the Gospel of Matthew that through caring for others and not being a sinner we'll be blessed by God and enter the kingdom of heaven. The only way to get to God, the preacher said, is to believe in and go through his Son, Jesus Christ. This leaves us in a quandary: Is the way to God's kingdom through caring for others and not being a sinner or is it through belief in Jesus Christ?

This contradiction is not to be taken lightly and can be a very touchy subject. I am not declaring here that being a good person and doing good deeds are the sole criteria for salvation. I am simply pointing out the contradiction between what the preacher said and what Jesus says in Matthew. The preacher's position that salvation is based on belief in Jesus is fully supported by the Gospel of John.

What has caused no end of trouble, debate, and conflict throughout the ages, and why this can be a touchy subject, is that Jesus' criteria for salvation in Matthew, Mark, and Luke is very different to what he says in John. We will discuss this more in the chapters to come.

While the sermon does its job by offering the way to redemption, it also epitomizes the doctrine of fear. For all its words it has but one message: You must go through Jesus Christ to be with God in heaven and spared from hell.

Why do preachers do this? I've often thought. Assumedly they've already accepted Jesus Christ as their Savior, and most of the people in their congregation have done the same. The answer, they would say, is they are making an argument for the people sitting on the fence (while bolstering the faithfuls' faith). With altruistic intention, they are passionately imploring souls to be saved. But where in scripture do we find the basis for all the fear linked to what we believe?

Consequences of Not Believing

Out of the nearly four thousand verses in the Gospels, there are only eight that specifically refer to there being consequences for not believing in Jesus, which have been commonly interpreted to mean you will go to hell (four verses will be addressed in this chapter and four in chapter 13). Relative to the text of the New Testament as a whole, this issue is hardly mentioned at all.

Our first example of a verse commonly bent to this purpose has caused great controversy over the ages and is still wreaking havoc today.

> Whoever does not abide in me is thrown away like a branch and withers; such branches are gathered, thrown into the fire, and burned. (John 15:6)

Having been conditioned to fear, all one has to do is glance at this verse, or hear it quoted (as it was in the sermon), to interpret it to mean: believe in Jesus or else...

To begin with, pay attention to what you think and feel when you read the word "fire." The association of fire with hell is so strong it might tempt you to accept the fear rather than search for the meaning. As with many verses in the Bible, however, it's possible that this one is not meant to be taken literally (as in, you will be thrown into a real fire). But even if there is only a small chance that the word fire is referring to hell, you might think, *why take the chance?* It's easier to just accept that meaning and believe as you've been told, so you'll be okay.

Can fire ever be just fire? Jesus did often use metaphors to get his points across. For that reason, the more familiar we are with the Bible and its language, the more data we will have upon which to determine context and meaning. Take a look at these beautiful verses from Luke, which also appear similarly in Matthew:

> Consider how the lilies grow. They do not labor
> or spin. Yet I tell you, not even Solomon in all
> his splendor was dressed like one of these. If
> that is how God clothes the grass of the field,
> which is here today, and tomorrow is thrown
> into the fire, how much more will he clothe you,
> O you of little faith!
> (Luke 12:27–28; Matthew 6:28–30)

In Jesus' time, grass was commonly burned in order to heat an oven—you threw it into the oven's fire. The phrase "thrown into the fire" in this verse refers to something transitory—the grass is here today, gone tomorrow—not the fire of hell. Just because thrown into the fire refers to judgment in one place does not mean it has to have the same meaning in another. These references to the transitory nature of life are common in biblical language.[1]

In another well-known verse of Matthew:

> You are the salt of the earth; but if salt has lost its taste, how can its saltiness be restored? It is no longer good for anything, but is thrown out and trampled under foot. (Matthew 5:13)

In other words, the salt without its flavor has no value and can be thrown away. If instead of "thrown out," Matthew had said, "It is no longer good for anything, but is thrown into the fire," the salt's flavor probably would have been equated with belief in Jesus for all the ages.

With these examples in mind, ask yourself, when Jesus spoke of branches being thrown into the fire in John 15:6, did his metaphor refer to your being thrown into an actual fire of hell, or did he mean something else? Seen with its preceding verse, he says:

---

1 "Grass" especially is used as a metaphor for transitory several times in the Old Testament: Psalm 37:2, 90:5–6, 102:11; Isaiah 40:6–8.

I am the vine, you are the branches. Those who
abide in me and I in them bear much fruit, because
apart from me you can do nothing. Whoever does
not abide in me is thrown away like a branch and
withers; such branches are gathered, thrown into
the fire, and burned. (John 15:5–6)

Taken together, if all you're thinking about in these verses
is the fear of hell, you are being distracted from two salient
points. First, every other time Jesus speaks of your being
thrown into the fire in association with judgment, he is refer-
ing to the day of judgment (and worth a reminder here, "hell"
(Gehenna) is not mentioned a single time in the Gospel of
John). Second, and more importantly, to focus only on the fearful, literal interpretation is to ignore a rich lesson offered. If
you're terrified of the dirt, you're not going to dig for the gold.

Jesus is speaking about having his spirit and his teachings
running through your veins (abiding in God) and what that
means for the strength and integrity of your being. Conversely,
without God's Spirit and teachings, you are a dried-up branch
connected to no vine—no source—which withers. And what
do we do with withered up branches and twigs? We gather
them and throw them away or burn them in our fireplace (and
branches in a fire eventually turn to dust and exist no more).

In other words, the point of the verses is to tell you the
value of abiding spiritually in Jesus and his teachings; they
are not about any external judgment or punishment for not
believing in him. The fire is there as a metaphor like everything

else in these verses—to convey a message. And, as you'll see when we get to the later chapters on John, Jesus speaks nothing there about any eternal fire connected with judgment, such as you've seen in the examples from the prior three Gospels. There are other verses in the Gospels that are similar to John 15:5–6, but because their metaphors do not involve fire, they are not as commonly appropriated to support the doctrine of fear. In the Gospel of Luke (and parallel verses in Matthew), Jesus says:

> I will show you what someone is like who comes
> to me, hears my words, and acts on them. That
> one is like a man building a house, who dug down
> deeply and laid the foundation on rock; when a
> flood arose, the river burst against that house but
> could not shake it, because it had been well built.
> But the one who hears and does not act is like a
> man who built a house on the ground without a
> foundation. When the river burst against it,
> immediately it fell, and great was the ruin of that
> house. (Luke 6:47–49)

Jesus relays this message other times using a variety of metaphors. Here he calls his teachings a good foundation on which to build our house. Are these words so different from those describing the branches that are full of spiritual life or dead inside, depending on whether or not they are attached to the main vine (the good Source)? He puts this yet another way in the Gospel of John: "I have come as a light unto the world, so that everyone who believes in me should not remain in the darkness."[1] And just as the house built without a foundation is destroyed when the river burst against it, so are the branches which are not connected to the vine destroyed in the fire.

Metaphors can often elucidate spiritual matters better than direct speech—in much the same way that poetry can at times communicate subtle ideas better than plain prose.

Obviously Jesus was not referring to our building an actual house, or to an actual river that would crash against it, or that without his light we wouldn't be able to read in the dark. But just as not everything he says is meant to be taken literally, not everything is meant metaphorically either. We must consider every example individually and decide what it means. It doesn't serve us to just accept what others tell us the words mean, and it can allow everything to get homogenized into a common mix that obscures what each verse means on its own.

The Reduction of Scripture

Absolutes are weapons used by the doctrine of fear, which wants to reduce all verses, whenever possible, to mean you either believe in Jesus or you don't, and, as a consequence, you are going either to heaven or hell. But the doctrine on its own has no power. It needs an ally to do its work. It needs your ego. It needs the part of you that must defend your being right—that doesn't want anything to conflict with what you've been told is the truth. Namely, that you are a being who is separate from God and, although God is aware of you, you

---

1 John 12:46.

cannot know God—not really—until you die, so you better believe rightly and be ready if death or the end of the world should come.

Your ego wants you to be comfortable in your separation; it wants you to feel safe so it can feel safe. It therefore keeps one of your greatest fears hidden deep within, yet influencing your thoughts—the fear that if you don't believe, you will burn—in order to keep you from searching further for spiritual truth.

Because this fear runs deep, your ego can lead you to believe that to even question a verse that is spoken by Jesus is to somehow deny Jesus. The implication is that to question anything is to question everything. But believing in what a verse means and believing in Jesus Christ are two distinct issues.

The divinity of Jesus Christ is not at issue here; the only issue is how certain verses are stripped of deeper meaning and used as absolute threats. Jesus' words offer us a vast amount of spiritual wealth and well-being if we can only free ourselves from being trapped by the belief systems and understandings from ancient times.

Your religion is obviously not a malicious body intending you harm. It is simply mired in the ghosts of its predecessors, who understood me only in terms of fear. These eternal threats of damnation can make you afraid to question what you've been taught.

You should question anything you've been taught. Re-search and seek the answers, in order to know for yourself whether what you've been taught is valid. You have nothing to fear and everything to gain in solidifying your faith through knowledge. Only your ego has everything to fear and everything to lose in your gaining knowledge that would help you break free of its dominion over you.

Our second example of a verse commonly interpreted to mean that hell will be the consequence for not believing in Jesus is found in the Gospel of Matthew (v.10:33). This well known verse of scripture was cited in the sermon I quoted earlier (the two other examples here are parallel verses of this teaching in Luke and Mark):

> Whoever acknowledges me before men, I will also acknowledge him before my Father in heaven. But whoever disowns me before men, I will disown him before my Father in heaven. (Matthew10:32–33)[1]

> Whoever acknowledges me before men, the Son of Man will also acknowledge him before the

---

[1] The preceding verse 10:32 was given for context; same with Luke 12:8.

angels of God. But he who disowns me before
men will be disowned before the angels of God.
(Luke 12:8–9)

If anyone is ashamed of me and my words in this
adulterous and sinful generation, the Son of Man
will be ashamed of him when he comes in his
Father's glory with the holy angels. (Mark 8:38)

Traditionally, these verses are taught to mean that if you
deny Jesus you won't get into heaven after you die, with the
further implication that you will go to hell—although the latter
goes *without saying*. Remember how strongly the doctrine of
fear can influence your understanding. As in the previous example, the doctrine's approach is an attempt to make whatever
scripture it can susceptible to this one interpretation (believe
or burn). Maybe that interpretation is true in this case. The
debates can never be settled, but there is the possibility that
its meaning could be similar to that of the verses about the
branches from the Gospel of John. There, by abiding in Jesus
your life would bear fruit; here, you benefit by acknowledging him.

If you want to accept the plain meaning that if you deny
Jesus you'll be denied entrance into heaven, there is still no
avoiding the fact that this verse refers to what will happen
on the day of judgment, not when you die, as you read about
in the previous chapters. This is clearly shown in the verse's
language in Mark. The 'Son of Man coming in his Father's

WHAT THE HELL IS HELL?

glory with the angels' is what heralds in our judgment and will end of the world as we know it.

Notice also in the verse from Matthew, Jesus does not say, "Whoever acknowledges me before men, I will also acknowledge him in heaven before my Father." He says, "I will also acknowledge him before my *Father in heaven*"—his common term for God in the Gospel of Matthew (meaning, my Father who is in heaven). In other words, whoever acknowledges Jesus before men, Jesus will acknowledge them to God.

❧❧❧❧❧❧❧❧

As we're beginning to see, the language Jesus used was usually not intended to be understood in cut-and-dry literal terms. As the good teacher, he employed metaphor and story in order to convey his paramount agenda that you should abide in God and love others (his two highest commandments), and that not doing so has consequences. He talks about those consequences in many other terms than a fiery punishment.

However, the most prevalent reason Jesus gave for going to *Gehenna* was sin. Sin is a major issue in scripture and we need to look further now into its meaning.

CHAPTER 10

SIN

Romans

The book of Romans, which follows shortly after the Gospels in the New Testament, is one of the letters written to nascent Christian churches from the apostle Paul, who spread the messages of Jesus in the first century. The letters, which are generally known as the Epistles of Paul, addressed various beliefs of the new Christian people, laying a foundation for, and disseminating the tenets of Christianity. Paul's writings are considered by scholars to be the oldest in the New Testament.

Romans includes a deeply invigorating exposition on sin, instructing you as to what it is and your personal responsibility to stay aware of it, while also prescribing the acceptance of Christ as the way to rise above it. In the sermon from the previous chapter, a couple of Romans' more popular verses were reduced to serving only the dogmatic, fearful teaching of Godly judgment. Let's take another look at how Romans was quoted there:

147

> The Bible says in Romans 3:23 that "all have
> sinned and fall short of the glory of God." Romans
> goes on to explain that the punishment for sin is
> death—separation from God in hell forever.

The preacher here takes the first verse from Romans 3:23 out of its context and attaches it to a second verse, which is from Romans 6:23, in order to support his own declared meaning: You are a sinner who is predestined for hell unless you choose Jesus to save you. As he later says, to deny Jesus is a capital sin as concerns your salvation.

The full statement, of which Romans 3:23 is a part, says:

> since all have sinned and fall short of the glory
> of God; they are now justified by his grace as
> a gift, through the redemption that is in Christ
> Jesus. (Romans 3:23–24)

These verses state what is said many times in the New Testament: Jesus Christ atoned for our sins—meaning that he paid the debt of our sins through his death. As it says in the Gospels of Mark and Matthew, the Son of Man came to "give his life as a ransom for many."[1] The verses from Romans do not, however, in any way define sin as not believing in him. Nor do they link not believing with hell.

As you read in the last chapter, the Gospel of Matthew

---

1 Mark 10:45; Matthew 20:28.

speaks a lot about sin and how it could land you in *Gehenna*. But there is a major difference between what Romans has to say about sin and what is written in the Gospel of Matthew. Whereas in Matthew you can choose through your actions whether or not to be a sinner, Romans states that you already are and have always been a sinner.

Romans features a definition of sin and redemption based on past and present, comparing Adam to Jesus. The state of grace (or glory of God) was lost through Adam's sin and continued evermore through successive generations. There is no getting around this fact, as the preacher reminds us in his sermon. You can be the most righteous person on earth. You can be a truly selfless soul whose only devotion is to helping others, but, as Paul says another way earlier in Romans, "All are under the power of sin, as it is written: 'There is no one who is righteous, not even one.'"[2]

In other words: everyone is a sinner. Sin is your birthwrong.

Romans tells us that when Jesus atoned for our sins it thereby allowed humankind to be restored to God's grace through him. The text does not say, "All sinners without Christ shall go to hell." However, it's not hard to see how anyone might assume that. It's the same old formulaic assumption we have already discussed, but it's worth repeating because there are few issues so vital to our well-being. As it has been laid out for so many of us: the Bible tells us in one place that there is a hell where sinners and evildoers will go (for example in Matthew[3]); the Bible tells us in another place (here in Romans)

2 Romans 3:9–10; Paul quotes Ecclesiastes 7:20.
3 "If your right eye causes you to sin, gouge it out and throw it away. It is better for you to lose one part of your body than for your whole body to be thrown into hell" (Matthew 5:29).

that sinners can be redeemed through Jesus Christ; then the math is done for you and what it adds up to is that if you don't accept Jesus Christ you will go to hell. This is, however, simply an assumption beyond what is written.

While Romans 3:23–24 says nothing about hell, it does say you are justified through God's grace and can be redeemed through Jesus Christ. If you shake off the negative assumption, the verses are saying something extraordinarily positive. They offer you redemption; with Christ comes everlasting good. This seems to be the important message Paul wants to convey here. Living a life in sin, apart from the grace of God, is suffering in itself, occurring while alive. Paul shows this when he says:

> For in my inner being I delight in God's law; but I see another law at work in me, waging war against the law of my mind and making me a prisoner of the law of sin at work within me. What a wretched man I am! Who will rescue me from this body that is subject to death? Thanks be to God, who delivers me through Jesus Christ our Lord! (Romans 7:22–25)

Romans 6:23, cited in the sermon, is a well-known verse from scripture and is another example of a verse that has commonly been used to induce fear. It states that "the wages of sin is death," which the preacher further defined as "separation from God in hell forever." This, however, is not what the verse actually says:

> For the wages of sin is death, but the free gift
> of God is eternal life in Christ Jesus our Lord.
> (Romans 6:23)

There is an important issue here we must know: the meaning of "death." The verse says the wages of sin is death, not hell. Death does not mean hell. If you read the whole chapter in Romans for context (or even the whole book), you will see that nowhere is death associated with any of the language we have taken as referring to hell that is found elsewhere in the Bible, such as an eternal fire or a lake of fire. Nor will you find the word hell in any of the verses that talk about death.

Death is a word that has two meanings, both of which are discussed in Romans. There is the literal meaning of physical death, but several times Romans also mentions a more profound spiritual meaning, which is that death is the state of being separated from God (or separated from the kingdom of God). Equating that separation with an eternal afterlife in a physical place of torment and suffering is, however, yet another leap beyond what is written.

Chapter 6 in Romans speaks about your spiritual life with or without Christ. Verse 6:23 says again what is found in the Gospels: with God, spiritual life is in you; without God, there is no spiritual life (death). It is not talking about an afterlife;

it is talking about your current state of being, based on your acceptance of God and his words, which, according to Paul in Romans, means based on your faith in Jesus Christ, his words, and his works.

"Sin" is usually thought of literally, as a wrongful or unrighteous act (defying God), which is harmful to ourselves or others. However, sin is another word that has a spiritual definition underlying its literal meaning. In this sense, it is anything that separates you from God. It is the act that puts you in spiritual death. (In its original Greek, "sin" is an archery term meaning missed the mark. If God is the mark, sin is hitting outside that mark.) By choosing sin in any of its many forms, you are denying the grace of God; you choose to be separate from God. This is not a choice whose repercussions come later. It is a choice that affects your life now.

If the ramifications of faith and righteousness, or lack thereof, occurred only after physical death (if, in other words, the spiritual realm were reserved for the afterlife), forgiveness of sin would not exist in the world. It would be waiting for you only after you died—if you had faith. And if you didn't have faith or lived in sin, you would not experience the consequences of that until you died. But scripture says the spiritual life is flowing through you. The question is, will you accept it or deny it? As soon as you heed the words of God, such as the lessons the Bible has to offer, and act on them, you tap into the spiritual life flowing through you and throughout the world. Deny the words—ignore the lessons—and you cut yourself off from that source. The price of sin is separation from God.

> To sin is to separate yourself consciously from
> Love. It is then your choice to feel judged, or
> outcast, and not a judgment from me. You
> need only choose more wisely going forward,
> in order to prevent your suffering.

Jesus says in Matthew, "If your eye is unhealthy, your whole body will be full of darkness. If then the light in you is darkness, how great is the darkness!"[1] If you choose a life of doing evil things (or thinking and acting in ways separate from God), you will live in the dark (separation is all you will know). You will experience more evidence that darkness is the truth, which in turn will strengthen the reality of the darkness for you.

How cutting yourself off from God might relate to any future judgment is another matter but, in Romans, Paul is quite clear about what will happen on the day of judgment and when it will be:

> But by your hard and impenitent heart you are
> storing up wrath for yourself on the day of wrath,
> when God's righteous judgment will be revealed.
> For he will repay according to each one's deeds:
> to those who by patiently doing good seek for
> glory and honor and immortality, he will give
> eternal life; while for those who are self-seeking

---

1 Matthew 6:23.

and who obey not the truth but wickedness,
there will be wrath and fury. (Romans 2:5–8)

Not only does Paul define God's wrath here in terms similar to those in Matthew's Gospel (the day of the final judgment), he also mirrors the essential message of God's criteria for judgment that Jesus preaches throughout Matthew, Mark, and Luke. Those who live a righteous life and do good will have eternal life, whereas those who are wicked and care only about themselves will incur God's wrath. Neither case is based on whether they believed in Jesus. However, Paul does speak later in Romans about faith in Jesus Christ as criteria for salvation.

⦿⦿⦿⦿⦿⦿⦿

Whether we want to believe judgment comes at the end of our life or at the end of the world, the notion that we have only two options: eternal life in heaven or eternal separation from God in hell, can mean that the only important teachings in the Bible are those pertaining to this frightening choice. It evokes the blinding temptation to close our mind and ignore the value of everything else written in scripture. Rather than studying the Bible and seeking to grow spiritually, we might become preoccupied with only those few sentences we are told will decide our fate.

The Bible does not exist simply to prop up a few key statements from God. Nor is it something we need to view as beyond our ability to comprehend. Rather, it is a text we can interact with. One of the reasons the Bible is eternally relevant is that its words are alive and speak to us intimately. We walk and talk with Jesus as though we were there. When he talks to his disciples, he talks to us. When Jesus advises someone how to find the kingdom of God, he advises us. His messages are intended to wake us up and make us aware of Spirit, not to put us to sleep and make us ready to be with Spirit when we wake from death in heaven.

No one can determine what is true for us all, but you have the power to seek God's truth for yourself. This is what Jesus taught. His mission was to make you aware of your potential and offer you a path to salvation. His messages were meant to ignite and propel your soul upwards. Having a relationship with God was/is for everyone. Keep searching for the highest good news. It is for you.

Listen to Jesus

In the Gospel of John, Jesus proclaims his purposes, among which are to make you aware of God, to show you that you can know God, and what this means for your life.

> Then Jesus cried aloud: "Whoever believes in
> me believes not in me but in him who sent me."
> (John 12:44)

> Believe me that I am in the Father and the Father

is in me; but if you do not, then believe me
because of the works themselves. (John 14:11)

There is a point made in the second verse that is easy to
overlook. Jesus is telling you: *Do not trouble yourself if you
cannot see who I am at this time. If nothing else, just look at
the things I've done and decide if you see God in them, and
if you do, believe in me.* If Jesus says (even once) it is okay
if you don't believe or know at the moment if he is one with
God, how can you allow anyone else to lay such absolute
threats of terrible consequences upon you if you don't believe? In his words, Jesus wants you to believe in him in order
for you to see God in and through him. He does this through
love, not fear and threats.

And if that one statement were not enough, Jesus gives
you more than you could ever have expected:

> Very truly, I tell you, the one who believes in me
> will also do the works that I do and, in fact, will
> do greater works then these, because I am going
> to the Father.[1] (John 14:12)

How could you ever do greater works than Jesus?

Because, rather than teach a belief system that would hold
you down, mired in the negativity of your limitations, Jesus
elevates you to see the unlimited possibilities in your relation-

---

1 Meaning he is going to be dead soon and back with God.

ship with God and your ability to do great works. Will you deny his words? How loving he is by passing on this most valuable information to you. Do you believe he said these things just to be a nice guy? He is telling you: *I'm leaving this world. Now it's your turn, and you know what? You will do things the world has never seen before—beyond what I did—because you are a unique person living in the world, now, who, through your faith, seeking, and perseverance, will build upon what has come before.* Jesus is humble while focusing on your potential greatness. So how could any religion created in his name have come to focus so heavily on your innate deficiency?

> Jesus promotes the truth of who you are,
> who you can be, and what you can do while
> alive. Your belief system, for all its good attri-
> butes, inadvertently assures you of who you
> are not and what you cannot do.

The doctrine of fear can cause you to become so deeply entrenched in the absolutes of "you either believe or you don't," that you might not realize there is another perspective: a doctrine of love. Leave all the debates about hell behind for a moment. Do you believe in God? Do you believe God loves you? What do you really believe about the nature of this God? Is he a God to fear or a God of love?

If you believe God loves you, and you believe God is perfect, would he have hidden the risk of your burning in hell when you die in mixed messages that could be saying one thing or another? All it would have taken is one or two sentences stating something like, "You shall know the everlasting fires of hell as soon as your life on earth ends if you didn't believe [the right belief]." Or, "Be careful not to live in sin, for if you die a sinner you will immediately go to the place of eternal fire and torment, where the devil and his angels live."

The essential question is, do you really suppose that a God who loves human beings as his children—who loves you—could ever sentence you to burn in an eternal fire? Setting aside grievous sin for the moment, do you suppose God would torture you eternally for any number of sins you might commit in one lifetime? If you have never committed a single sin, if you did nothing but help the poor, sick, and needy, but you didn't believe the right beliefs, would God drown you in a lake of fire forever? Even if God were to dispense such eternal punishment, what would be the point? How would that benefit you or God?

As you get swept up in the drama of absolutes—accepting as a given that the doctrine of believe-or-burn is true—you don't stop to examine what's behind that choice or where it came from in the first place. Even if you believe that it's only evildoers who burn in hell for eternity when they die, again, why would God bother (he's never going to see them again)?

One thing is certain: one of the greatest fears people had two thousand years ago—God's judgment and punishment—is alive and thriving, relatively unchallenged to this day.

Have we not come of age to let go of these beliefs? Are the dark ages not over? Can we be the generation to break free of these ancient fears? Can we cleanse our spirituality—our relationship with God—of all the negativity?

CHAPTER 11
LOVE

The Gospels are filled with many more positive lessons and messages than those few verses that have been exploited to support the doctrine of fear. It would take too much space here to list all the words of love, light, guidance, and wisdom in the Gospels. Instead, I have listed some of the catch-phrases from these numerous verses. They are verses you can ponder for a lifetime, glean new meanings as you grow, and grow with the new meanings. You can feel love and learn about love through these words. Even if you are not very familiar with the Bible, you will probably recognize many of these sayings, because they have permeated our culture for centuries. Instead of just scanning the list, actually read each line to yourself.

Love God.[1]
Love your neighbor.[2]

Mt=Matthew; Mk=Mark; Lk=Luke; Jn=John
(1) Mt 22:37; Mk 12:30; Lk 10:27. (2) Mt 22:39; Mk 12:31; Lk 10:27.

You are the light of the world.[1]
Let your light shine. [2]
Love your enemies.[3]
Bless them that curse you.[4]
Pray for those who abuse you.[5]
Pray for those who persecute you.[6]
Do good to those who hate you.[7]
If you are angry with a brother or sister, you will be liable to judgment.[8]
Be perfect [in your love], as your Father is perfect.[9]
Love one another as I have loved you.[10]
If anyone strikes you on the cheek, turn the other also.[11]
Do not judge, so that you may not be judged.[12]
Do not condemn, and you will not be condemned.[13]
Ask and it will be given to you.[14]
Seek and you will find.[15]
Knock and the door will be opened to you.[16]
Do to others as you would have them do to you.[17]
Be merciful, just as your Father is merciful.[18]
Forgive, and you will be forgiven.[19]
The truth will set you free.[20]
Those who humble themselves will be exalted.[21]
If you have faith you can move mountains.[22]
Don't be afraid, just believe.[23]

---

(1) Mt 5:14. (2) Mt 5:16. (3) Mt 5:44; Lk 6:27. (4) Lk 6:28. (5) Lk 6:28. (6) Mt 5:44. (7) Lk 6:27. (8) Mt 5:22. (9) Mt 5:48. (10) Jn 15:12; 13:34. (11) Mt 5:39; Lk 6:29. (12) Mt 7:1; Lk 6:37. (13) Lk 6:37. (14) Mt 7:7; Lk 11:9. (15) Mt 7:7; Lk 11:9. (16) Mt 7:7; Lk 11:9. (17) Mt 7:12; Lk 6:31. (18) Lk 6:36. (19) Mk 11:25; Lk 6:37. (20) Jn 8:32. (21) Mt 23:12; Lk 14:11.(22) Mt 17:20; 21:21; Mk 11:23; Lk 17:6 (though Luke uses "Mulberry tree" instead of mountain). (23) Mk 5:35.

With God all things are possible.[24]

Whoever does not receive the kingdom of God as a little child will never enter it.[25]

Whatever you ask for in prayer with faith, you will receive.[26]

Give, and it will be given to you.[27]

So do not worry about tomorrow, for tomorrow will bring worries of its own.[28]

Most of these phrases, which are intended for your practical spiritual instruction, come from the first three Gospels (Matthew, Mark, and Luke), each of which has its own messages and perspective on Jesus' life and ministry. As you read them, however, you find they also have common themes, similar stories, many of the same sayings, and are laid out in basically the same order of events from beginning to end. For this reason, the first three Gospels are often referred to as the Synoptic Gospels. *Synoptic* comes from a Greek word meaning "seen together." You can easily compare them to see how alike they are and also where they are different.

The consensus of Bible scholars is that Mark is the oldest Gospel (written about forty years after Jesus died) and is the source for much of the material in Matthew and Luke, which is also why the three Gospels are so similar (Matthew and Luke were written ten to fifteen years later; and John about ten years after that).

---

(24) Mt 19:26; Mk 10:27; Lk 1:37. (25) Mk 10:15; Mt 18:3; Lk 18:17. (26) Mt 21:22. (27) Lk 6:38. (28) Mt 6:34. (29) Most of the messages about loving others are found in Matthew and Luke.

In the Synoptic Gospels, Jesus hardly mentions what you ought to believe about him. Rather, he talks a great deal about the value of your faith in God, the importance of loving others,[29] and the numerous ways you can learn more about the kingdom of God.

The Gospel of John is fundamentally different from the Synoptics in that it does tell you what you need to believe. It centers on the divine identity of Jesus Christ and the salvation you'll gain from believing in him.

In the previous two chapters we discussed the few messages—some of them beyond the scope of scripture—that our religions have focused on and, inadvertently or not, have instilled the doctrine of fear. In this and the following chapter we will focus on the themes of love and seeking that are found in so many of Jesus' messages. All of his words discussed in these chapters are found in the Synoptic Gospels. The Gospel of John will be the subject of the chapters that follow them.

There are many themes in the Synoptic Gospels and many complicated issues related to what Jesus said and did and the interpretation of his words. This discussion of them is not meant to be blindly idealistic or to make the argument that these themes of love and seeking are the only words to which we should pay attention. Rather, it is to provide you with an overview of how often these positive themes occur throughout these Gospels. But, more importantly, to draw your attention to how powerfully the messages resonate with you, and have resonated with us collectively, in order to indicate the weight they deserve to be given in our understanding of what the ministry of Jesus was about. They will show that love was the heart of him, the impetus behind most of what he said and did, and will demonstrate his desire for others to learn about and enter the kingdom of God.

Several times towards the end of Jesus' ministry in the Gospel of John he directs people to love one another, and he also talks throughout the Gospel about God's love, but in the Synoptics we get much more of a discourse about the practical ways we should act and live in order to be loving people.

When you read through the list of phrases earlier, did you understand what each one meant? For fun, try to answer this question out loud: What does it mean that you are the light of the world? Or, why will the humble be exalted?

These are spiritual messages, as are the others on the list. Perhaps you agree they are the words of God. Spiritual messages are understood intuitively. For example, in the first saying, you may intuitively understand that "light" refers to your goodness. To let your light shine in the world is to bring joy to the world with your love, your smile, your good will to others. Over time, your own life experiences can contribute to the depth of meaning the words have for you personally.

As for the humble being exalted, you probably know that being humble is a virtue. This saying is a loving instruction because being humble will help you to learn, to grow, and to know God. Humble people don't think they know everything. They are ready to learn. Humble people are open to receiving spiritual information. Those who think they know everything have no room to take in anything new. Because they believe they already have all the answers, they miss what information God might have for them. This can lead to all kinds of pain and failure that being receptive to God's lessons might have averted, which is why the entire verse reads, "All who exalt themselves will be humbled, and all who humble themselves will be exalted."[1]

Your understanding of spiritual words is enhanced by the knowledge you gain through your personal experience with Spirit (or your personal relationship with God). Let's say, for example, that one day you saw an old man struggling to carry his groceries to his car. Without thinking about it, you immediately went to help him. Afterwards, as you watched him drive away, a deep pleasure swept through you. You learned that helping someone in need feels good—your satisfaction came from the other person's benefit. Henceforth, you have the spiritual knowledge that there is reward in caring for others. Perhaps you will also have realized that this is the kind of world you want to live in. You understand better why Jesus preached for us to love our neighbor.

Jesus knew we are beings of love and that when we treat other people with care we are living in harmony with our true nature. We may have to choose and act according to that nature, but that doesn't make who we really are as beings of love any less true.

We can debate biblical interpretation, religion, or philosophy, but no matter whether the teaching came from God or is something we learn for ourselves, love suits us. It feels good to hold open a door for someone. It feels good to help someone in

---

1 Matthew 23:12; Luke 14:11.

need. It feels good to love others. It feels good to be loved. "Be kind to one another"[2] is a teaching we can all feel in our hearts to be righteous—whether we are religious or not, and whether or not we believe in God. But, of course, all of this is only true for each of us who endeavors to be what we generally think of as a good person—someone who cares about others.

There are certainly people who care nothing about others, who choose to care only about themselves, and who, in the extreme, do egregious harm to others, with no sense of remorse. And from basic selfishness up to the worst sins, there are costs, and people suffer accordingly—obviously first and foremost anyone who is harmed, but that harm is also reflected back upon the harmer in who they are, even if they are unaware. In a sense, everyone's punishment for not being a good person is being themselves, which is another reason why Jesus emphatically urges people to be caring and righteous.

He said there would be a final assessment of us; who we are will be revealed in full and our fate decided accordingly, but that doesn't mean the results of who we are don't also manifest now. Being an evil person is often marked by an underlying isolation and misery, just as being a loving person is often rewarded by feeling good and joyous.

Jesus teaches you how to spread love in the world. He tells you how to practice loving your neighbor as yourself (i.e., how to live in harmony with who you are), and how to

2 Ephesians 4:32.

do what you are told is God's will in the world: forgive others; be merciful as God is; don't be angry with others; don't judge people; treat others as you would have them treat you.

You are told to be perfect in your love as God is in his. Normally, you love your family and others who love you. But Jesus says that to be perfect in your love you must also love your enemies or those who harm you. "You have heard that it was said, 'An eye for an eye and a tooth for a tooth.' But I say to you, Do not resist an evildoer. But if anyone strikes you on the right cheek, turn the other also;"[1] and, "You have heard that it was said, 'You shall love your neighbor and hate your enemy.' But I say to you, Love your enemies and pray for those who persecute you."[2]

He tells you in Luke, "Do not condemn, and you will not be condemned."[3] If you condemn someone else, that is, judge them or treat them poorly, you are also condemned because you are then choosing darkness. If you don't condemn others, neither will you be condemned. There is a model for moral righteousness and godly behavior laid down in these Gospels, and that model is founded on love.

These are messages to which everyone can relate. The love Jesus preaches about is for all. Maybe that is why his teachings have taken such deep and lasting root in our culture. Everyone is equal in Jesus' eyes, and all are called to be righteous.

What lies at the heart of righteousness, he says, is for your actions to be driven by virtue. "When you give to the poor do not tell anyone; do not let your left hand know what your right

---

1 Matthew 5:38–39.

2 Matthew 5:43–44; similarly said Luke 6:27.

3 Luke 6:37.

is doing."[4] He wants you to help people for the right reason—because you want to help them—not to gain approval.

"When you pray, do not do so in order to be seen by others."[5] "When you fast, do not look somber and visibly suffer such that others know you are fasting."[6] He wanted you to be genuine in all things, not to be doing the right things for the wrong reasons.

In Luke's parable of the good Samaritan, Jesus highlights the value of mercy while also defining its purity.[7] He tells the story of a man who has been beaten and robbed and lies half dead at the side of the road. Note that he says a priest saw the man and passed him on the other side of the road. A Levite (a temple assistant from the tribe of Levi) also passed by the man. But a Samaritan, who was an outsider, came along and felt pity for the man, tended to his wounds, and took care of him. It is this man whom Jesus prizes, because he is the one who showed mercy to another. Love and goodness here are defined by one's actions and what is in one's heart, not by one's religious status.

Your faith in God is one part of who you are; your actions are another. Neither one is meant to negate the importance of the other. It does not devalue faith to say that good deeds are not dependent on faith. There is a love that shines through these teachings that is not reliant on your beliefs about who Jesus is. The values he espouses are based on the authenticity of your spiritual/social practices. Are you truly a righteous person; do

4 Matthew 6:2–4.
5 Matthew 6:5.
6 Matthew 6:16.
7 Luke 10:29–37.

you care for others; do you desire to live in a righteous world and stand up for what's right—for loving others?

This is not to imply that belief doesn't also matter. In fact, the relationship between your belief and your salvation is the most repeated message in the Gospel of John. However, it is equally important to remember that this is not the focus of the first *three* Gospels of the New Testament at all. Their messages should at least not be slighted as less important than faith.

In the Synoptic Gospels, Jesus did not burden you with complicated details about what you ought to believe theologically; he wanted you to know there is a God, and that love is the way to his domain. "Come to me, all of you who are weary and are carrying heavy burdens, and I will give you rest. Take my yoke upon you, and learn from me; for I am gentle and humble in heart, and you will find rest for your souls. For my yoke is easy, and my burden is light."[1]

<hr />

A good way to wrap up this short summary of the loving teachings found in the Synoptic Gospels is to look at Jesus' love of children. He says, "Let the little children come to me; do not stop them; for it is to such as these that the kingdom of God belongs. Truly I tell you, whoever does not receive the kingdom of God as a little child will never enter it."[2]

Jesus is saying we should all strive to be humble, to maintain an open mind, and to have a joyous heart. It is the purity of

---

1 Matthew 11:28–30.

2 Mark 10:14–15. Similarly said in Luke 18:16–17 and Matthew 18:3.

the children that Jesus adores (relative to God we are all little ones at any age). This message is important enough to have been mentioned in each of these three Gospels. Were you ever lit up inside as you watched children laugh and play? "For it is to such as these that the kingdom of heaven belongs."[3] There is no mention or intention in these words that our relationship with God should be governed by fear.

At what age do we teach children that if they think the wrong thoughts they could be condemned to hell for all time? It seems a complex matter and a sinister concept for a child to bear. Are we as adults any more ripe for abuse?

The good news is that there is a kingdom and Jesus wants us to enter it. The Synoptic Gospels provide an instruction manual for the soul, and define the actions and values required to make us ready to receive the kingdom. All of these actions, ideals, and intentions, we can categorize as love—our choice to be loving, caring people, or, in other words, to follow our heart. But Jesus teaches about another complementary aspect of our humanity we are to embrace if we want to find and enter the kingdom of God, and that is through seeking. In addition to following our heart, we need to use our mind.

---

3 Matthew 19:14.

CHAPTER 12
SEEKING

The first words out of Jesus' mouth in the Gospel of Mark are an exhortation to believe the good news: "The time is fulfilled, and the kingdom of God has come near; repent, and believe the good news."[1] What is the *kingdom of God* and what does *has come near* mean? Is the kingdom a place that will come into existence at the end of the world with the return of the Son of Man? Is it a place that was temporarily on the earth while Jesus lived? Is it a place we go to when we die? The kingdom can be interpreted to mean different things at different points in the Bible, and perhaps there is a lesson in that: The phrase "the kingdom of God has come near" has deep-reaching spiritual implications that are like buried jewels waiting for us to dig and find.

Jesus provided a multitude of parables in order to help us understand the kingdom. As a reminder, a parable is a story that conveys a lesson or truth beyond the literal meaning of the words. For example, the parable of the good Samaritan

---

1 Mark 1:15. An alternate translation is the kingdom is *at hand.*

we discussed in the prior chapter, which shows that mercy and goodness are more important than one's religious status. Or the parable about building a house on the solid rock foundation of Jesus' words instead of on the ground without a foundation. We can use these parables to assist us in gaining spiritual knowledge. But Jesus made them purposefully mysterious: we must find the meaning of the stories on our own, in order to get that knowledge. The following are excerpts from some of Jesus' parables.

The kingdom of God (or heaven) is like:

seed sown on good soil, which bears fruit a hundredfold[1]
a mustard seed that grows and becomes the greatest of
    all shrubs[2]
a small amount of yeast that is mixed into flour and
    leavens it[3]
treasure hidden in a field that someone sells all
    he has to buy[4]
a pearl of great value that a merchant sold all
    he had in order to buy[5]
a net cast into the sea that caught fish of every kind; they
    kept the good but threw out the bad[6]
a bridegroom for whom virgins kept their lamps lit all
    night, not knowing when he would arrive[7]
a wedding banquet to which all are invited[8]

---

(1) Mark 4:20; Matthew 13:23; Luke 8:8.
(2) Mark 4:31–32; Matthew 13:31–32; Luke 13:19
(3) Matthew 13:33; Luke 13:21; "leaven" means to make dough rise.
(4) Mt 13:44. (5) Mt 13:46. (6) Mt 13:47–48. (7) Mt 25:1–13; similar saying Lk 12:36–40. (8) Mt 22:2–10.

If we strictly held to the final judgment discourse found in the Synoptic Gospels, which we discussed in prior chapters, most of these metaphors found in the parables would refer to the kingdom to come when the world is transformed with the return of the Son of Man. In that case, the kingdom being near would mean it was due to arrive soon. Jesus says in Mark, "Truly I tell you, there are some standing here who will not taste death until they see that the kingdom of God has come in power."[9]

In the Gospel of Luke, however, there is a spot where Jesus appoints seventy-two followers to go out in pairs "ahead of him to every town and place where he was about to go."[10] He tells them to proclaim, "the kingdom of God has come near."[11] It seems in this case Jesus is indicating that he embodies the kingdom and when he is near, it is near.

Nevertheless, when it comes to scripture, it's possible that ideas are not as straight-forward as they seem, and there are deeper meanings to be found.

Many millions of people still believe that Jesus will return within their lifetime, bringing about the end of the world as we know it.[12] Today, however, the most popular view among people who believe in a kingdom of God is probably that it is a spiritual realm we will enter after we die. If we have

9 Mark 9:1; parallel verses: Matthew 16:28; Luke 9:27 with slight variation.

10 Luke 10:1.

11 Luke 10:9; parallel verse: Matthew 10:7.

12 Close to 76 million American believe Jesus will return to earth by the year 2050, according to: "Jesus Christ's Return To Earth," Pew Research Center, Washington D.C. (2010); https://www.pewresearch.org/fact-tank/2010/07/14/jesus-christs-return-to-earth/

accepted Jesus Christ as our Savior we will enter the literal kingdom of heaven.

My experience, however, has been that we can begin to know this kingdom, this place of God, this realm of Spirit while we are on earth. Said another way, we can understand what Jesus meant by the kingdom by using our own spiritual experience and development as a reference. Perhaps that is what Jesus meant when he said some would not taste death before seeing the kingdom come—if we follow his teachings, seek and ask to find the kingdom, and live the righteous life he prescribes, we will indeed find the kingdom while we are still alive.

There are many English translations that read, "the kingdom of God is *at hand*," or have a footnote about it. Perhaps that expression does a better job to convey the spiritual implications of the words—meaning, the kingdom of God is within our grasp—it is here for us now to find.

Many of these metaphors are open to different interpretations, as well as have universal truths that can apply to more than one area, regardless of the original intention. That is why the kingdom can be understood a variety of ways, as you saw earlier. For example, seen sown on good soil producing a hundredfold could mean that Jesus' words will result in many entering the kingdom when judgment day comes. Or, early Christian missionaries took it to mean they were spreading the seeds to make Christianity grow. Or, the words planted within us lead us to live righteous lives and to have good harvests in our spiritual lives, our health, relationships, or even our work.

While none of us can declare that our understandings of

his parables are definitely what he meant, see if the following explanations resonate as true with you.

In the first metaphor on the list, Jesus speaks of the seed that fell on good soil and produced a hundredfold. This is one of the few parables he actually explains to his disciples: "the seed is the word of God (or word of the kingdom)."[1] The good soil refers to those who "when they hear the word, hold it fast in an honest and good heart, and bear fruit with patient endurance."[2] In other words, you receive (read or hear) the words of God, and as you reflect on them and come to understand them, their wisdom transforms you for the better. The hundredfold crop produced is your spiritual bounty in a realm called the kingdom of God (going forward I will sometimes call it a kingdom of Spirit).

In another verse, Jesus compares the kingdom of God to a mustard seed that, when planted and tended, grows into the greatest shrub. This means when you harbor even the smallest seed of spiritual knowledge within you, you can, by watering it with your attention and seeking, grow and evolve as a spiritual being.

I believe we can see the metaphorical truth of this parable manifested in the Synoptic Gospels. When you read Mark's Gospel, you find it is the most terse. It tells the story of Jesus' ministry—the events, miracles, interactions, and his teachings—in a more basic manner than Matthew's and Luke's.

Most of the verses I've mentioned so far, which focus on love and how you should treat others, come from Matthew and Luke, and are progressions from the basic teachings in Mark.

---

1 Luke 8:11; Matthew 13:19, respectively; Mark 4:15 "the word."
2 Luke 8:15; Mark 4:20; Matthew 13:23.

For that reason, I can't help seeing the seed of the kingdom in Mark's material as having blossomed in Matthew and Luke. Perhaps we could continue to let the kingdom blossom with the understandings we have today, and in generations to come.

It could also be that Jesus' seed coming to fruition applies both to the individual and to the bigger picture of the kingdom to come. Just as destruction that comes from sin applies to our current lives as well as a final judgment.

In another parable's metaphor, the kingdom is like a net cast into the sea. Think of all the books you've read, or all the spiritual teachers you've heard speak, as the sea into which you cast your net. The good fish are the messages of wisdom and truth you retain, which in turn transform you for the better, the bad ones you should throw out. In like fashion, the text goes on to say, "So it will be at the end of the age. The angels will come out and separate the evil from the righteous."[1]

Or, think of yourself as a merchant seeking pearls. The great pearl you find is your growth in spiritual understanding and the expanding love you give, receive, and feel as a result, which would be worth selling all you own to buy.

Jesus' many parables relate to the kingdom of Spirit in different ways, thus providing you with a variety of options to assist your understanding. They are themselves good seed. A parable is only mysterious if you don't understand what it means, and then you have a few choices. You can accept that

1 Matthew 13:49.

you don't understand it and turn away. You can ask someone to explain it to you, although you might then understand the explanation without internalizing it, which means you might not benefit from it, or, even worse, the person you ask may give you the wrong explanation. Or, you can think about what the parable means, search within, use your intuition, and figure it out. Seek the kingdom, ask for understanding, knock on the door because you want it to open.

As you start to better understand the kingdom through understanding one or more of Jesus' parables, metaphors, or other spiritual messages, you find that it becomes easier for you to understand others. In Matthew (and similarly in Mark and Luke), when the disciples ask Jesus why he speaks to the people in parables, he answers, "To you it has been given to know the secrets of the kingdom of heaven, but to them it has not been given.[2] For to those who have, more will be given, and they will have an abundance; but from those who have nothing, even what they have will be taken away."[3] This is the law of abundance and applies to many areas. In this case, the understanding of Jesus' words will reap more of the same—an exponential growth in your understanding. No understanding, with no desire for understanding, will yield only less understanding.

* * *

Jesus' words were meant to help us become better people.

---

2 Matthew 13:11; similarly said in Mark 4:11 and Luke 8:10.
3 Matthew 13:12; similarly said in Mark 4:25 and Luke 8:18..

Not only did he want us to love God and love other people, he also wanted us to have an active spirituality and grow in understanding of it. Yet many of the denominations that have developed in his name have contradicted his words and prioritized only the command to worship him. It's as if the great humility Jesus showed in the first three Gospels—teaching us about love, God, our spiritual potential, but rarely about his own divinity—was not taken as sincere—as if we don't think he really meant it when he was likening us at all to himself in terms of our ideals and spiritual potential. Believing in Jesus Christ took precedence over all the other teachings in the Gospels—leaving that material in a distant second position. The second position material made for good and useful Sunday sermons I've heard, which surely helped guide us in our lives and are the basis of Christian values, but it all amounted to not much, relative to the fundamental requisite of belief.

A preacher might believe he is being humble and serving us because, he says, only Jesus knew God intimately, and only through belief in Jesus can we get to God. (Let's take as a given that the preacher is genuinely loving and doing what he thinks is right to help us.) But how is it being humble for any of us to discount such a fortune in messages in the words Jesus spoke? How in light of these three Gospels, which embody so much love, did we ever come to reduce Jesus' teachings to a single dogmatic and fearsome ultimatum: believe or burn?

How in the richness of all his teachings did we reduce them even to the most glorious promise of: believe in Jesus and you'll go to heaven? Even if nothing could sound more purely good, and even if we take hell off the table, if we believe the good news (the gospel) is simply that we can believe in Jesus and go to heaven, we are living in denial of a soul-level fear beneath the surface: if we don't believe in Jesus we will not go to heaven. We are still saying, "Believe or else."

Or is it any better to say, "Believe, but only evildoers will go to hell"? What happens to all the good people who didn't believe in Jesus...I mean *exactly* what? It can make us uncomfortable to think about such things, but it shouldn't. Is that what Jesus would have wanted?

For many years something gnawed at me—burned in me. Something didn't feel right. God was being used, slighted, misappropriated to serve the agendas of those who wanted their beliefs about God and their interpretations of scripture to be accepted by everyone else without question.

Stepping aside for a moment from biblical interpretation, based on what I knew of God from my own spiritual life, God did not threaten. God did not use fear as leverage to acquire souls. God did not reserve love only for those who believed the right belief, or thought a certain way, or said the right words.

Jesus seemed to want to fill me with love, while for so long I was taught to have my faith driven through fear. This was not an overt campaign of old-school fire and brimstone, and it's not that those I heard preach didn't stand for love (that feeling of love is something I always cherished and what drew me in to Jesus' words in the first place). And more and more there seems to be a shift towards keeping love in the forefront of practicing faiths. But the threat of judgment and the exhortation to be prepared for the next life is always there, whether unspoken for an entire sermon or rarely mentioned by anyone outside of church, stoking an eternal fire of fear that undermines love no matter how lovingly we dress it up or how lovingly we act.

Near the end of the New Testament there is a small book called I John,[1] which contains a few wonderful messages that seem to be among the most purely inspired by Jesus' teachings:

> God is love, and those who abide in love abide in God, and God abides in them. (1 John 4:16)

> God is light and in him there is no darkness at all. (1 John 1:5)

> There is no fear in love. (1 John 4:18)

Jesus seemed to want to empower me through love to find the kingdom of God, yet I was being taught submission. Based on what I'd learned about the ego, I could sense it was up to its old tricks—making itself comfortable and safe. My preacher's ego, my ego, and the egos of those around me at church all seemed to have the same agenda: don't question any of this stuff too much; accept what you are told. The collective fear made each of our own fears seem normal; together we accepted our place of separation from God. We all believed God created our religion, so who among us should question God?

This left a disconnect between Jesus' telling me to seek God, which meant asking questions, and my being told at

---

1 The "I" means First John, not to be confused with the Gospel of John.

church to simply accept what I was told. Why was I being led away from searching for answers?

> The preacher taught that you are a separate being, but this is how you can feel comfortable as a separate being: "Accept Jesus Christ so you can go to heaven when you die and then be together with God." He wasn't out to harm you or prevent your spiritual growth—his love was sincere. He was doing the best he could. But someone taught him, just as he taught you. His sermons were as much about helping himself to find peace as a separate being as they were genuinely intended to help you.

A New Way to Discern which Words are God's

When it comes to the interpretation of what it says in the Bible, the debates can be endless. Perhaps a good way to determine which are truly the words of God would be to see how their results are or were manifested in the world. Would it be fair to say that if any of God's messages limited your spiritual growth, fulfillment, or happiness, it would be a good indication that the source of those words was not God, or that the words or their meaning got altered along the way from their origin to you? Or, if you were taught anything that prevented you from loving others—such as judging them for believing differently from you or imagining them to be condemned—would you agree that is different from what

Jesus originally taught? Perhaps almost all the spiritual words you've been taught were actually God's, but if men added or altered even a small number of them, their meaning could go astray. A pot of delicious soup can be ruined by adding even a pinch of the wrong spice.

If Jesus said you can know God and find the kingdom of God yourself, and you are unsure if God is actually in your life or if you are living up to what's possible for you, hasn't something gone awry somewhere between what he said and what you've been taught?

If Jesus preached a ministry of love, but you are being given reason to fear, isn't something wrong?

> Remember, your belief system is a construct of men. Even if a man teaches you the Word of God, he is a man. He is imperfect. He is not the Word. He is not God. If he tells you ninety-nine things that are correct, that doesn't mean one thing he tells you can't be wrong. Be careful. You live in an ego-dominated world, and where ego and ideas about God interact, conflict is inevitable. What should you do if an ideological conflict occurs between you and what you've been taught to believe? Will you just ignore it—be afraid to question what you've been told because it could cause you eternal harm?

You are taught that God's words are perfect, and if you have any trouble understanding them, or you disagree with any of them, or you find contradictions among the perfect words, it is because you are a mere imperfect person. You are told that if you can't find the truth of the words yourself it's okay—just accept what you're told they mean. This is another ruse of the ego. It is to your ego's advantage if you don't quite understand God's words and stay in your place, removed from the study and knowledge that would provide you firsthand authority in spiritual matters. A separate being, in separate understanding, looks for validation in being separate; your ego wants you to believe that your place in this life is to remain separate from God and it will try to support that position in whatever way it can.

But if God wants you to find him, he could not want for you to remain separate from him. He could not mean for you to fear him, or to fear questioning him, or to fear questioning anything. If God is love, he could not want you mired in the fear of condemnation. Let's now take a look at where all the talk specifically about condemnation comes from.

CHAPTER 13

THE GOSPEL OF JOHN

Unlike its three Synoptic predecessors, in which Jesus' ministry focuses on righteous behavior as criteria for judgment, his central message in the Gospel of John is to believe in him in order to have eternal life. It contains some of the most beautiful and spiritually profound verses found in the Gospels, yet it also contains some of the most powerful verses that have been interpreted and used to support the doctrine of fear. Those interpretations, however, take great liberties with the actual words in the Bible, which could well mean something different from what many of us have been told.

In chapter 9, we went through four of the only eight verses in which we see consequences directly related to not believing in Jesus. The other four are in the Gospel of John. The following is perhaps the most often cited verse to support the belief that we are damned to hell if we do not believe in Jesus as the only Son of God:

> Whoever believes in him is not condemned, but
> whoever does not believe stands condemned

already because he has not believed in the name
of God's one and only Son. (John 3:18)

What does "condemned" mean? The word itself means
receiving a negative sentence or judgment. In this verse, believers can agree it is God's judgment. But does condemned,
as it appears here, mean sentenced to hell, or is it referring to
something else? It is most commonly understood as referring
to hell, even though the word hell is not mentioned once in
the Gospel of John.

On its own, out of context, it's easy to deduce from the
verse that we're damned to hell for not believing in Jesus.
To make that meaning work, however, we have to look at
the words isolated not only from what Jesus says in the three
preceding Gospels (where hell is not once equated with not
believing in Jesus) but also from one of the primary messages
in the Gospel of John: that whether Jesus is talking about condemnation or salvation, he is almost always concerned with
our present lives, not the afterlife. I will show this through
scripture. How condemnation or salvation relate to the afterlife is another matter, which Jesus addresses in only one
passage in the Gospel of John when he speaks of his followers
going to an afterlife heaven.[1] There is not a single verse, however, where he speaks of an afterlife condemnation.

John 3:18 has three sister verses that also say we will be
condemned in some way for not believing in Jesus.

---

1 John 14:2–4, which will be discussed in a later chapter.

> Whoever believes in the Son has eternal life,
> but whoever rejects the Son will not see life, for
> God's wrath remains upon him. (John 3:36)

> I told you that you would die in your sins, for
> you will die in your sins unless you believe that
> I am he. (John 8:24)

> The one who rejects me and does not receive my
> word has a judge; on the last day the word that I
> have spoken will serve as a judge. (John 12:48)

As these four verses are commonly understood to share the same meaning that we will be condemned for not believing in Jesus, let's address them all by addressing John 3:18. Here is the verse again for reference:

> Whoever believes in him is not condemned, but
> whoever does not believe stands condemned
> already because he has not believed in the name of
> God's one and only Son. (John 3:18)

Jesus is speaking in the present tense. He does not refer to a future judgment and say, "Whoever believes in him *will not be* condemned." He says, "Whoever believes in him *is not* condemned." He does not say, "Whoever does not believe *will be* condemned." He says, "Whoever does not believe stands condemned *already*."

As you read in the previous chapters, scripture can often have profound and experiential meanings beyond the literal understanding of the words. John 3:18 is not merely speaking about an either/or choice—believe or don't believe and x or y will happen in the future. Rather, Jesus is making a statement about who you are—what your belief or lack thereof says about you.

The verses convey a spiritual understanding that if you do not believe in who the Son of God is on earth, it means you don't recognize God, which means you don't know God— don't have a relationship with God—and that, in and of itself, is the condemnation. If, on the other hand, you do believe in the divinity of the Son of God on earth, it means you do recognize God, because to some degree you have a relationship with God, which you can believe and be guided in, and that keeps you from being condemned.

Jesus is saying, as he does throughout the Gospel of John, that your personal relationship with God is what keeps you in the light. If you can't believe in God on earth—abide in him and learn from his teachings—you are in the dark—spiritually dead—you isolate yourself and are separate from God. In John, this pertains to your life, not what comes in the future.

> I have come as a light unto the world, so that everyone who believes in me should not remain in the darkness. (John 12:46)

Those who abide in me and I in them bear much
fruit, because apart from me you can do nothing.
(John 15:5)

Whoever follows me will never walk in darkness
but will have the light of life. (John 8:12)

I am the bread of life. Whoever comes to me will
never be hungry, and whoever believes in me will
never be thirsty. (John 6:35)

To *bear fruit* or *do nothing* or *walk* or *never be hungry or
thirsty* are earthly matters—metaphors pertaining to the present. These verses are variations on the predominant theme of
the Gospel of John—salvation and condemnation in the present. To believe that condemnation refers to an afterlife place
where you will suffer eternal, physical torment is to believe
something Jesus never says and actually defies what he does
say throughout John.

However you want to interpret John 3:18, by the words
alone, stating that one is condemned for not believing in Jesus
Christ is not the same as saying that one will go to hell for it.
This is further clarified in the very next verse:

This is the verdict: Light has come into the
world, but men loved darkness instead of
light because their deeds were evil. (John 3:19)

WHAT THE HELL IS HELL?

This line doesn't get cited nearly as often because it detracts from the power held in the doctrine of fear. Here Jesus plainly refers to a condemnation on earth, not after death. The judgment occurred *before* men were made aware of the light that is Jesus, not after. They were condemned already "because their deeds were evil;" they could not see the light because they "loved darkness," and so were condemned again when the light presented itself. They continued their cycle of darkness.

Now look at the verse that directly precedes John 3:18. Here Jesus says:

> For God did not send his Son into the world to condemn the world, but to save the world through him. (John 3:17)

> but whoever does not believe stands condemned already. (John 3:18)

He is saying in the first verse, "I'm not here to condemn you." Then why would he turn around in the next verse and mean to say, "But believe in me or you're condemned to hell"? That literal meaning wouldn't make sense; he can't be here to condemn you and not condemn you at the same time. In John 3:17, Jesus says he came to save you (save the world). He does not then contradict himself in the next verse because it is not he who judges you, nor is he referring to future punishment, but rather it is just you who stand condemned already in your life now by not believing in him, according to the Gospel.

The verses of John 3:17–19 are spiritually profound, and

it takes time and contemplation to understand them. Keeping in mind the explanations you've just read, read the group of verses together now:

> For God did not send his Son into the world to condemn the world, but to save the world through him. Whoever believes in him is not condemned, but whoever does not believe stands condemned already because he has not believed in the name of God's one and only Son. This is the verdict: Light has come into the world, but men loved darkness instead of light because their deeds were evil.
> (John 3:17–19)

The verses say: Jesus did not come to condemn; belief in him determines who is (now) condemned or not; here's why men were condemned already. To quote the middle verse (John 3:18) without the context of the verses that surround it allows its meaning to be misconstrued as referring to a future judgment and to a place God might send you (believe or burn). The only meaning that works in the context of all three verses taken together is that the condemnation he refers to is the present earthly state of those who are unable to see and believe in who Jesus truly is.

Now, it could be said that condemnation in life is logically followed by condemnation after life, but if Jesus meant we would go to hell, why would he be cryptic about it? Why did he not say, clearly and directly: "He who has not believed

in me shall be condemned to hell"? Or, "He who has not believed in the only Son of God shall be condemned to eternal
hell after he dies"? Jesus did not say these words, but long
after he died men attached this meaning to the words he did
say. Who are we going to believe?

Please consider these issues the next time you feel threatened by hearing or reading John 3:18. It can be easy for any of
us to simply accept that what we've been taught is supported
by the Bible. But we can do the research for ourselves. The
words are all sitting right there in black and white and red.

If we want to stick with the literal meaning of condemnation as referring to a place where we could be sent, we still
need to deal with the fact that, as we've discussed in the previous chapters, when Jesus speaks about a time for that judgment,
he is talking about the final day at the end of the world, not
after our death. This is not one of the mysteries of the Bible
we have to dig for; it is written throughout the Gospels.

Jesus refers to the final judgment in the Gospel of John
as well, when he will return to judge the living and the raised
dead (although minimally; it's called "the last day" in John).

> The one who rejects me and does not receive my
> word has a judge; *on the last day* the word that
> I have spoken will serve as a judge.
> (John 12:48; emphasis added)

> This is indeed the will of my Father, that all who
> see the Son and believe in him may have eternal
> life; and I will raise them up *on the last day.*
> (John 6:40; emphasis added)

It is important to note that whereas the Synoptic Gospels and John may differ on the criteria for salvation, there is one thing all four Gospels can agree on: there will be a day of final judgment for humanity. This is mentioned elsewhere in John, but his ministry is not based on it, as it is in the Synoptic Gospels.[1] Whereas in the Synoptics, Jesus talks about *Gehenna* or fire as punishment for the wicked on that day (or the outer darkness), in the Gospel of John, he almost exclusively talks about condemnation occurring in the present for those who don't believe in the only Son of God. However, he tells us nothing about what any punishment will be for those people on the last day, or where they will be going.

All that Jesus tells us in John about what happens on judgment day to those who were condemned is that when the Son of Man comes, "all who were in their graves will hear his voice and come out ... and those who have done evil will rise to be condemned."[2] Notice in this verse, the condemned who died are dead—in their graves—not in any hell, and even more worth paying attention to, it is those *who have done evil* that will rise to be condemned, not those who didn't believe. And they will be condemned on the last day when all the dead are raised.

---

1 John 5:25–29, 6:39, 6:44, 6:54, 11:24.
2 John 5:28–29.

———————❧—————————

We have now been through all the biblical information relevant to the doctrine of fear (believe or burn). It serves us to note there are 3,779 verses in the four Gospels[1]; just over half of which are the words Jesus speaks. Out of those verses, there are only four that say we will be condemned for not believing in him, and there are four others that say there will be a consequence of some sort if we don't believe in him. As we've now seen, those verses have often been quoted to threaten us with hell for not believing, yet not one of them mentions or has anything to do with an afterlife hell. That fact, having been verified, should technically eliminate the doctrine of fear once and for all from our minds, and knowing that doesn't take away the spiritual meaning of believing and not believing in Jesus. Regardless, eight verses out of 3,779 verses have been driving this doctrine of fear for all these ages.

Astounding, isn't it—what we have allowed? Our fixation on a relatively small object in our spiritual field of vision has blocked the full grandness of the light—like the sun eclipsed by the moon. Moving past the fear, we can now focus our attention on the primary belief that resulted in that fear.

Believing Only in Jesus

Your belief system revolves around your needing only to believe in Jesus. Yet Jesus did not

———————————

1 Give or take a few, depending on which translation you use.

point to himself as the principal object for your attention. Jesus spoke of all power coming to him from God.

As Jesus says elsewhere in John:

Very truly, I tell you, the Son can do nothing on his own, but only what he sees the Father doing; for whatever the Father does, the Son does likewise. (John 5:19)

Do you not believe that I am in the Father and the Father is in me? The words that I say to you I do not speak on my own; but the Father who dwells in me does his works. (John 14:10)

Then Jesus cried out: "When a man believes in me, he does not believe in me only, but in the one who sent me." (John 12:44)

I can do nothing on my own. (John 5:30)

These messages are repeated several times in John.[2] So why does the same Jesus who wants you to know that if you don't believe in *him* you are condemned, also tell you that

2 John 6:38, 7:28, 8:28, 12:49, 14:28.

everything he teaches and does comes from a higher authority? If Jesus himself says the Son is nothing without the Father, then belief only in the Son is not enough. Likewise, to not believe in the Son alone is not enough to condemn you; that involves the deeper meaning about who you are that can't see God. He was giving us spiritual instruction that we could recognize God through him; not threatening us to believe solely in him or be damned.

The message of Jesus drawing your attention to God (the Father) rather than himself is attested in the Synoptic Gospels as well:

> As he was setting out on a journey, a man ran up
> and knelt before him, and asked him, "Good
> Teacher, what must I do to inherit eternal life?"
> Jesus said to him, "Why do you call me good?
> No one is good but God alone." (Mark 10:17–18)

> But Jesus looked at them and said, "For mortals it
> is impossible, but for God all things are possible."
> (Matthew 19:26)

That Jesus called your attention to God as the principal Source is not to say that he didn't also want you to be aware of his own spiritual identity. There is no message in John repeated more than Jesus telling you to believe in him for eternal life, and sometimes he tells you just to believe in his words.

> I tell you the truth, he who believes has everlasting life. (John 6:47)

> but those who drink of the water that I will give them will never be thirsty. The water that I will give will become in them a spring of water gushing up to eternal life. (John 4:14)

> that everyone who believes in him may have eternal life. (John 3:15)

> Very truly, I tell you, whoever keeps my word will never see death. (John 8:51)

> For God so loved the world that he gave his one and only Son, that whoever believes in him shall not perish but have eternal life. (John 3:16)

I've counted twenty-four such statements in the Gospel of John. In very few instances, however, do these positive statements also mention a negative judgment if you don't believe. That's an implication we easily make, which contributes to the reduction of scripture into simplistic two-choice terms; if you're not saved you must be damned. But as you've now seen, the question of salvation or condemnation has much greater depth than whether we are going to heaven or hell.

Then why is it that we take the few verses threatening a negative judgment, such as John 3:18 or its three sister verses, and empower them to be as important as the hundreds of other verses Jesus spoke in the Gospel combined?

Why must all positive statements about salvation be considered to imply the alternative possibility of condemnation, even when condemnation is not hinted at in the verse itself? Indeed, why must the entire good of Jesus' ministry—all the promises of salvation and all the teachings of ethics, values, and how to be a good person that fill up most of the pages in the Gospels as to what Jesus said—only work if the greatest fear is invoked with it?

It's because the separate being sees things as a reflection of its own separation: there can't be eternal life without there being eternal death; we are either with God or without God; we are separate now, but we can be with God later; those who don't believe now will be separated for eternity. This is all separatist thinking.

The ego likes things to be simple; it likes yes or no answers—we either believe or we don't—the rest of what's written in the Bible doesn't matter all that much to the ego. The idea that believing or not believing could lead to anything other than simple corresponding results (heaven or hell) does not compute for our ego—or so it would have us believe. Our ego wants to preserve our status quo, and this two-choice belief system assists that purpose by leaving us no reason to seek further. But if the richness of Jesus' teachings is all boiled down to mean that for now we need only believe or not believe, and any judgment comes later, our spiritual life of seeking, in between, is rendered insignificant.

What is Hell?

We have now covered what Jesus says in the four Gospels about the way sinners, evildoers, or those who don't believe in him will be judged. To recap, the Gospels of Matthew, Mark, and Luke speak of a time when Jesus will return to the world to judge all of humanity. The judgment will be based on who we were and how we treated others, not on our belief in Jesus (judgment based on belief comes in John). He will come in the clouds with power and glory. There will be fire and destruction and he will end the world as we know it. This will be the day of judgment, the hour of the apocalypse.

At that time, God will rid the world of all sin, sickness, pain, suffering, and even death itself, creating a new kingdom of God on earth, where the righteous will receive blissful eternal life. The unrighteous (sinners and evildoers) will be sentenced to an actual place on earth, located just outside of Jerusalem, called *Gehenna* (the original Greek term from the New Testament, which most English Bibles have translated as "hell"), where they will be thrown into God's fire and destroyed. There are also times when Jesus refers to the fate of the unrighteous ending in fire but he doesn't mention a location (like *Gehenna*), or, a few times he says they will be thrown into "the outer darkness." No one is thrown into *Gehenna* when they die; it only happens on the day of judgment.

All of the above is based on a literal interpretation of

scripture. The only other option is to believe that all of Jesus' talk about *Gehenna* or fire was meant to be understood metaphorically. Perhaps Jesus was conveying spiritual messages through the use of the apocalyptic language at times.

Whatever the case may be, Jesus knew *Gehenna* was a real place and that, according to the Old Testament, it was a desecrated site where people had practiced the abomination of child sacrifice by fire in worship of a pagan god. But even if we choose to believe that Jesus used the same name *Gehenna* to refer to an entirely different place of fire and torment, existing in another dimension (or, as some believe, in the depths of the earth), he still never says that we could go there when we die, or because we did not believe in him.

As for judgment based on belief, which we discussed in this chapter, only in the Gospel of John does Jesus speak of a condemnation of those who don't believe in him, and they are condemned in the present—to walk in darkness while they are alive, rather than in the light. There is no afterlife condemnation discussed in John. We have only the few verses where Jesus mentions the "last day" (John's term for the day of judgment), and he does not tell us anything about what will happen to to those who are raised to be condemned.

In conclusion, if we believe in *Gehenna* as a literal hell, the Bible says it is on earth, outside of Jerusalem, and the unrighteous could be sent there only when Jesus returns to carry out God's judgment of humanity and end the world as we know it, where they would be destroyed in God's eternal fire.

But that's not how we traditionally define our hell.

Instead, whatever we believe is the reason for why we would end up there, our conventional definition of hell is a place we could go when we die, to burn in fire for all eternity. Therefore, what did Jesus say about hell as we define it? Nothing. Our concept of hell is not found in scripture; it was invented long after Jesus died.

．

⟨decorative divider⟩

Of course, all we have of Jesus' words is scripture. None of this is to say that Jesus did not know there were afterlife ramifications for evildoers, the unrighteous, or even for those who didn't believe in God, but he said nothing about that in the Gospels—at least not in any literal sense. However, as we've discussed, the language of Spirit often has a greater depth of understanding below the surface meaning of the words. Jesus may very well have been speaking in metaphorical terms about *something* we could think of as a hell. But, as we've now seen, if it is believed that the Bible is the perfect literal Word of God, the fiery afterlife we call hell does not exist.

This then begs the question, if this version of a hell is not in the Bible, how is it that we ever allowed ourselves to be taught and believe in it?

The answer is not hard to see, except for our ego that might not want us to see it, and it does not affect anyone's faith in Jesus or God one iota to admit it: We *chose* to believe that this afterlife hell of everlasting fire and torment was in the Bible—that is, the early Christian bishops and theologians did, beginning approximately a century after Jesus died, and then we passed it down faithfully through so many generations that it solidified as being factual truth.

The doctrine of fear that came out of that was simply an error. We have four Gospels, written by four authors, at different times over a thirty year period. In Matthew, Mark, and Luke, we saw a place called *Gehenna* where sinners and evildoers would be sent and we took it to be hell. We saw in John that if you don't believe in Jesus you are condemned. Then we mashed them together to come up with the doctrine: if you don't believe in Jesus you will go to hell.

Based upon everything we've discussed about the ego, we can see how easily we locked that belief into place. In order for our ego to maintain our inner security, sometimes it is more important for us to defend and be right in our beliefs than it is to ask questions and possibly jeopardize that security, even if the answers provide the actual truth.

For that reason, the core tenets of the belief system, of which hell is a major part, had to be powerfully stated as absolutely correct from the beginning, or else the whole system could be wrong. We had to believe it's either all true or none is true—yes or no. Those were, and still are, the only two choices given. We have a God or we do not; we either believe in him or we don't; we have a heaven or a hell; we will go to one place or the other when we die. In each case there is no in-between.

That type of thinking can cause us to perceive even Jesus in over-simplified, binary terms—he is the Lord or he is not, and his humanity can seem unimportant outside of that. It is as important to understand who Jesus was as a living man in order to understand his teachings. One of the best avenues to take for doing this is to delve deeper into a term used often for Jesus in the Gospel of John—the Son of God.

Jesus is called the Son of God in the other Gospels as well;

however, the Gospel of John offers us great insight into the meaning it gives to the term. As we'll see in the next chapter, this is not a simple matter either, much as we might like it to be for our ease of understanding.

CHAPTER 14

THE GOSPEL OF JOHN PART 2: THE SON OF GOD

The words Son of God are usually taken literally to mean that Jesus is the Son of the Father (God). But the Son of God is also a spiritual term requiring spiritual understanding. The part of Jesus that we call the Son of God is his spiritual being. One way to look at the name Jesus Christ, in this understanding, rather than a literal one, is to say that Jesus is the name of his human self, and Christ represents his spiritual being. Christ is the Son of God, living through the man Jesus.

The Son and the Father share the same spiritual nature. If you recognize one, you recognize the other; "And whoever sees me sees him who sent me."[1] The term Son of God describes a relationship to God—the spirit within Jesus as it relates to the Spirit of God. It is the flame of a candle as it relates to a bonfire—the same substance, so to speak, to a lesser degree. It is Jesus who tells us this in the Gospel of John.

---

1 John 12:45.

WHAT THE HELL IS HELL?

While the Son and the Father are of the same spiritual essence, such that Jesus said, "The Father and I are one,"[1] he also knew that "The Father is greater than I."[2] It is in the living example of his duality as both the Son of God and a man that we can learn to understand who we are, which is the only true path to discovering for ourselves who the Son of God is.

Recognizing the Son is a subtle awakening. We cannot know the Son merely by worshiping the Son. We believe in the Son and thereby accept that the Son is real, but rather than believing that the Son of God is outside of us somewhere, perhaps in heaven, we come to know who and what the Son is through knowledge of our own spiritual being—our soul, which shares the same nature with the Son. But like the Son to the Father (or the candle to the bonfire), there is a distinction of degree in our relationship to the spiritual being of Jesus, as the Gospel shows him to be.

The term *self-realized* has long been used in eastern religions to refer to one who has been spiritually awakened—one who lives in conscious awareness of the truth of who she or he is—a spiritual being enrobed in flesh. This person has gained knowledge of God and actually lives according to spiritual lessons learned (that is, walks the walk). Spirit lives through this person, who talks and acts in a godly manner. Such a person has, for example, realized the wisdom of love—they know how it feels and how it fulfills both them and those with whom their love is shared, and express that in how they live and treat others every day.

To say the Son is a realized spiritual being means the

---

1 John 10:30.
2 John 14:28.

spiritual being is awake in reality (real-ized)—his or her light shines in the world. Jesus said, "No one after lighting a lamp puts it under the bushel basket, but on the lampstand, and it gives light to all in the house."[3]

To say that Jesus Christ was the *fully realized* spiritual being on earth is to say he was the fully realized Son of God—the perfect Son—God in the flesh—shining perpetually—Spirit living fully in the world through a man, as is written of him. Or, in other words, the living God.

Accept for the moment that Jesus did mean you were in the dark and already condemned on earth if you could not believe he was the Son of God. This means if you can't accept the truth of a spiritual being who could be fully realized, you are also denying the spirit in yourself; for if you can't accept the truth of the one, how can you possibly accept the truth of who you are and your own potential? That lack of acceptance can keep you from realizing your truest, highest identity, which would lead to your most fulfilled life. And the ignorance of who you are might also lead to much suffering, as you make mistakes and don't know why, or even that you are making them, and cause yourself or others pain, which could lead to an unfulfilled life. That is a form of the condemnation.

Further, if you can't at least believe in the possibility of who Jesus was, and thereby deny the possibility of who you are, you are kept from knowing God as well as you could. For if you don't believe you share the same nature as God, you have no reason to look within yourself as a means to know God better and to live in the realization of that knowledge—you are spiritually stifled. You cut yourself off from the spiritual life

---

3 Matthew 5:15; parallel vs Mark 4:21; Luke 11:33.

of God that flows through you (you cut yourself off from the vine). Therefore, when Jesus said whoever could not believe in the Son of God is condemned, he was also saying you could not believe in yourself.

There are, however, many who would say that Jesus was not speaking in such general terms and he specifically meant that anyone who did not believe in him as the *only* Son of God would be condemned.

Jesus as the Only Son of God

The identity of Jesus Christ as the only Son of God is the core belief of all religions conceived in his name; he was the Messiah—the one and only—and it is only through his unique divinity that we can be saved.

If this is the most important belief for us to have, isn't it odd that he is never called the *only* Son of God in Matthew, Mark, or Luke, all of which speak of him as the Son of God but not as the only Son? John is the only one who repeatedly makes that distinction, and he does it four times:

...as of a father's only Son... (John 1:14)
...It is God the only Son ... (John 1:18)
...he gave his one and only Son ... (John 3:16)
...in the name of God's one and only Son. (John 3:18)

Regardless of what we believe, endless debate, prejudice, hate, torture, and even killing have resulted from those words.

Throughout the ages and up to the present time, crusades, inquisitions, pogroms, and innumerable other systematic practices of harming, suppressing, ostracizing, seizing of property and possessions, stripping of rights have been perpetrated against people who held non-Christian beliefs. How did any church or nation ever end up with a creed of: "Accept the eternal loving light of the only Son or we'll kill you"?

If you look at the manifest results of biblical words, or their interpretation, as an important part of the criteria for determining whether or not they are actually God's words, something is wrong with the "only" verses of John. If those four verses are indeed God's words, would it be fair to say the words have been grossly misinterpreted? Think about the kind of man Jesus was when he lived, what his ministry was about, and decide if you think it could have been Jesus' will for people to be harmed in his name.

Very often these atrocities have been excused by saying that, at the time they were perpetrated, people didn't know any better, and surely there have been cases throughout history when perpetrators were ignorant and thought they were justified. It's more likely, however, that people did know better and used those exclusionary words as a religious justification for their actions against whomever they deemed to be enemies or whose interests were not in accordance with their own.

Your religion knows better now in that it does not physically harm those who don't believe.

> However, it still proclaims that the rest of the world's people who do not hold its same beliefs are condemned. This is an issue your religion deems outside of its hands—regardless of the results in the world, or that it works against love by outcasting others. The voice of your religion says, "It's not our fault that people choose not to believe the truth of the one and only way.[1] Let's focus on the good those words have done, continue to do, and all the people they have helped to save."

The words calling Jesus the only Son of God have indeed done much good in the world. The strength of the language has drawn countless good, caring people to God and Jesus. However, there is no degree of good that offsets the reality of the bad. While we need not dwell on the harm that has resulted from those particular "only" words throughout history, should we just ignore it? Is it possible there could be powerfully good meaning in those words, yet also something wrong with them? Could the perfect words of God result in the torture or death of millions of people…or even one?

If we agree that the words of God should not result in people's being harmed, and we believe that Jesus is "God's one and only Son" are, in fact, the words of God, then something must be wrong with any interpretation of those words that

---

1 About 70 percent of the planet's population—roughly 5.5 billion people—who are not Christians.

brings about the horrific results listed earlier. Only a faulty source—words that are not God's or a misunderstanding of God's words—could produce such grievous harms.

It is written: "A bad tree produces bad fruit. A good tree cannot produce bad fruit."[2]

Can you think of any harm that has come from the words "love your neighbor?"

John 14:6

In the arena of philosophy, even the most religious-minded might engage in friendly debate about Jesus' being the one and only Son and what that might mean. There is, however, another verse in John stating more directly that Jesus is the only way to God. The most serious gavel slams down, as the statement is used to render all debates obsolete.

> Jesus said to him, "I am the way, and the truth, and the life. No one comes to the Father except through me." (John 14:6)

This is perhaps the most boldly, authoritatively, and frequently cited verse of gospel, often put forth as the single most definitive statement from God declaring that Jesus is the only way. End of discussion.

The verse does have immense spiritual value, and we'll be discussing its meaning in a later chapter. For now, however, I

---

2 Matthew 7:17–18.

want to point out that, as with the words "only Son of God," if we believe "except through me" are the words of God, something is wrong with any interpretation of those words that not only brings about the harms cited earlier but also denies us the freedom to question or explore other possible avenues to God or for better understanding. We never know what other means God might have in order to help our understanding, and seeking elsewhere doesn't mean we are turning our backs on our faith.

Part of why this verse becomes imperial and stifling to other messages is it has often been taken out of context and interpreted as a self-contained truth when, in fact, it is embedded in a chapter rich with discourse about Jesus, God, and the Holy Spirit.

In chapter 14 of John, Jesus emphatically wants us to know and believe in God. By doing so, he says, we will come to recognize the Father in the Son and the Son in the Father. If we can believe in the Son, we can believe in ourselves and, as he says, we can do the works he did and even greater works, and the Son and Holy Spirit will always be with us. Perhaps those statements can all lend to the understanding of *why* Jesus is the way, the truth, and the life, in a more profound and tangible way than simply "because he is the Son of God."

Unfortunately, historically and to the present day, our tendency has been to isolate John 14:6 and quote it as a stand-alone pillar of Godly command. We can sometimes see it quoted on a banner hanging off the railing at a football game, or on a boxer's trunks, or on a billboard on a highway. While everyone has the right to love whatever verses of scripture they choose, the undeniable reality is that the tendency to isolate and elevate this verse has amplified the words *except through me* and given the verse a significance beyond all others. The unfortunate result has been to make it seem that scripture has only one critically important thing to say. In addition, and perhaps more tragically, the acceptance of this verse as the only truth that matters has set people against one another rather than encouraging them to love one another.[1]

It's a single verse that, for roughly over sixteen hundred years since the Bible was put together, has kept a great many people from digging deeper into biblical meanings or seeking other sources of enlightenment. After all, what's the point of looking elsewhere if Jesus is the only way? What's the point of even reading the Bible if that is all we need to know? Like it or not, believing that's all we need to know has resulted in many millions of us who believe in Jesus but have no need or desire to read the Bible or learn more about it, because it's much easier to simply accept what we've been told, and thereby get to heaven.

If we know that all of these exclusionary concepts have caused no end of fear, people's being actually harmed throughout history, and walls' being built to separate one group of believers from another, why is it so hard for us to explore what might be inaccurate about our interpretations of such words? What is it that keeps us dead-set on interpreting so many verses of scripture in simplistic and literal terms, regardless of how the consequences play out in individuals or the world? The answer is plain to see: Our religion dictates specifically how the Bible's words are to be understood, no questions asked.

---

1 "I give you a new commandment, that you love one another" (John 13:34, 15:12, 15:17).

The Power of Religion

Let's turn back the clock some sixteen to eighteen hundred years to the fourth century when the canon of the New Testament was beginning to be solidified and Christianity, which became the official religion of the Roman Empire, started to take hold worldwide. Over the centuries there have been major (and minor) breaks from the original doctrines and practices that have resulted in the many thousands of denominations today. But, for the moment, let's pretend we are in a continuation of that religion today so that we can discuss it in a more objective and relatable way. You'll no doubt recognize some of the following generalizations that still apply to many of our denominations today, as well as to some other religions in the world.

This foundational religion preaches in absolutes. We have to believe either all the words of its scripture or none of them. We can't pick apart scripture sentence by sentence.

When did God say that?

God didn't. The religion did. Inadvertently or not, it removed the incentive for us to think independently.

This religion tells us that its words are the perfect words of God. Then it tells us that to question those words is to question God.

It's a quick sleight of hand. Who said this religion was made by God? The religion did.

This religion said God said this religion is God's. Did you catch that? The religion says that to deny the religion is to deny God. Think about the logic.

God may be in any of our religions, but only our ego could

have a need to declare that our particular religion is made solely by God. This way there's no need to question anything.

In its beginning, this religion said that God inspired its doctrines. Somewhere along the way, however, human egos got in the way of our endeavoring to write down God's words. The religion had the words of Jesus, but the religion was governed by men (the bishops at the time), and putting together the scripture was a collaborative effort on their part. They had a vast number of writings and oral accounts to sort through in order to determine which were most likely the words of Jesus. This didn't happen in one sitting but took place over the decades after Jesus died, through intense debates and conflicts concerning all sorts of issues, from minor questions of diet to the most major questions of theological interpretation. It actually took centuries to arrive at an overall consensus—a winning side—and consolidate all those writings and oral accounts, which they deemed right, into one collection of books that would be deemed the authoritative canon 'til kingdom come.

When the work was finished, this religion held it aloft as its inspired scripture. But over time, the religion then shifted from talking about "God-inspired words" to "the words of God"—absolutely. The entire text collectively came to be regarded as perfect, "the Word of God." The religion went from human beings' inspired and noble efforts to transcribe God's words to declaring that the words went straight from God to the page, into one infallible book. At that point, the religion departed from truth—departed from reality—and now, these many centuries later, we have been made to fear questioning it all.

God tells us to seek the truth for ourselves. This religion tells us to accept its truth blindly.

God encourages our questions. This religion does not.

It welcomes questions that help lead us to its answers, but those answers may not be questioned.

There's no denying how much the world has benefited from the words, the works, and the spiritual force of Jesus Christ, or that those three gifts were made everlastingly accessible due to people believing in his resurrection. Whether you have been saved, spiritually educated, guided, enlightened, or just enjoy Christmas, the goodness resulting from Jesus is apparent. The spiritual identity of Jesus has not been called into question here—only our understanding of his words.

Can we, with all genuine reverence, and without diminishing one cubit of Jesus' stature, extend our toe onto a new path of understanding? Can we discard the fearful thinking that says to change the way we think is to negate or dishonor the past? Can we dare to suggest that our religions are not perfect?

In most areas of our development as a people, we move toward greater enlightenment and even mock the ignorance of our past. We once believed that the world was flat, that leeching was advanced medicine, and flying was for the birds. Yet, when it comes to our religious beliefs, we maintain a death grip on them as if we were wrapped around a pole a thousand feet off the ground to keep from falling.

Clinging to ancient beliefs is not simply a matter of faith;

it's a matter of fear. It's fear of what will happen if we question God. It's fear of what happens when we die. These fears long preceded Jesus. People feared God from the moment they were able to formulate the idea of God.

Jesus emphasized that we have a God to love and a God who loves us. If we had pursued that love exclusively, rather than creating new fear, we might by now have looked on fearing God the way we view ancient people who feared that a comet or an eclipse signaled the end of the world.

If ours is a God of love, and Jesus is his Son, why has there been, and why is there still, so much fear related to our beliefs in him, as well as negative judgment towards others with different beliefs?

Can we boldly turn our gaze toward the possibility that *something* might be wrong with the way we understand Jesus' teachings? Call Jesus perfect; I will not deny you. Can you admit we are not perfect?

The spiritual identity of Jesus and the grandness of his teachings are the highest worth for a lifetime of seeking to understand. The more we grow in that understanding, the more we evolve as spiritual beings. This is an open-ended education to infinity, and one that grows richer in love with each season of seeking and practice of his universal loving teachings.

The quite finite study, such that it's contained within these pages, is to know that our common beliefs about hell are not supported by the Bible, although they are usually taught to us as having come from it. You have now seen all the evidence as to what Jesus said about hell. You have seen what it means to believe or not believe in him, according to the Gospel of John. The age-old fear of hell has been fueled by our simply not questioning what we've been told to believe. There is no need of any blame; only love. It was only natural to fear hell when we're taught from early childhood that the stakes of our faith are us going to heaven or hell. The fear of hell made us not question hell.

This information is not easy to process all at once, and you have read the culmination of what took me many years to come to understand through countless hours of research and personal seeking. My hope is that you may benefit from those labors, gain the information in a short period of time here, and be able to verify everything that was said here for yourself.

Still, to question any lifelong belief raises greater challenges than the mere processing of information, and it can be fearful, arduous, and even difficult in your personal life. My suggestion is to not fall prey to the thought that to question anything is to question everything. You can parse out the topic of hell without it interfering with your faith in Jesus or God.

You might believe that if any Bible verse even possibly threatens condemnation for not believing in Jesus as the only Son of God, it suffices as a cause for fear. If so, I would urge you just to make sure you research for yourself what that verse is actually saying or what it means, and not to do yourself the injustice of not weighing everything else Jesus had to say. Allow yourself to consider the possibility that you can be saved without the implied threat of eternal condemnation. And if you at least determine in your studies that the condemnation

Jesus spoke of is not an actual afterlife place called hell, consider that condemnation is simply not salvation, and perhaps that is hell enough.

> Most harms that have ever come, involving the name of Jesus, through the minds and hands of man, for almost two thousand years, come down to a single cause. It has been in our midst all along—in your religious beliefs and at the heart of what hasn't felt right to you for so long now.
>
> It is the crux of one line that has kept you from seeking the truth for yourself and let only your religion tell you what the truth is. For too long, one word has put the cap on that curious open space inside you, which yearns to learn and know.
>
> There is one single word forged by your religion—by the human ego—which transformed the meaning of everything Jesus taught. In so doing, it transformed Jesus in the psyche of your religion. This one word, posing as a testimony of faith, has done more to put Jesus out of your reach than all the years of your religion have done to bring you to him.

Have you figured out the one word?

PART III

CHAPTER 15

ONLY

This chapter contains the bulk of the original material I wrote down in my car that day, as well as some new material that came years later when I sat down to write this book. Unlike any other chapter, it is written entirely in the voice that spoke to me.

The voice grows more powerful here. It is more direct. As a reminder, when the text here says "you," it is referring to me—to my thoughts and experience with the beliefs I'd wrestled with for many years. Yet, even as I heard it, I sensed that it was also talking through me to whomever else would be willing to listen and might benefit from the words.

You'll have read some of these messages in earlier chapters, the difference being that you will now be seeing them in their original form, uninterrupted. I hope everything you've read up to this point will enhance your understanding of them.

Finally, I experienced this voice as a powerful, sustained impulse of messages, which I wrote down as quickly as I could.

But I am just a flawed human being after all—not a perfect medium. Any time God's words came to me it was through the filter of my life's experience and my ego (striven though I have to transcend it), and often using my own detailed experiences and understandings to communicate. I believe that is how God speaks to all of us.

Where does that leave you in terms of trusting me or this source? Where it always should: to decide for yourself which are the words of God and which are not. There are no writings in the world that should be above scrutiny.

As a reminder, sometimes the voice spoke in the first person ("I" or "me"), and sometimes in the third person ("God"). There is no disparity in this. I learned over time that certain messages were better relayed in the more objective sense of the third person, and I also didn't want to change any of the original words.

<hr/>

My words are not meant to dictate the truth in a forceful manner, but rather to provide an opportunity for you to learn through them. If you can accept there is a Holy Spirit at work here, it is critical to the process that you be honest with yourself. For the moment, allow yourself the indulgence of believing it is I, God, who speaks to you.

Remember, "God" is just a word. You could just as well call me a guide, speaking through a man. How do you suppose I could reach you if not through

a medium you were capable of understanding—
through your own humanity?

Please check the cloak of your religion at the
door and hear these words through your own
divine spirit and love of God. Keep an open mind.
Put aside preconceived notions concerning God.
Try to reserve judgments if they rise.

If you can't accept I am God, then ask the
God you know, "If there is anything written here
that you would like me to take in, let me know."

When I say, "remember" something, I am
offering you a lesson. You will notice my lessons
are filled with love—as I am—and are not about
fear. Be careful of those who teach you to fear—
be wary of those lessons. Fear is man-made.

If you can accept this fundamental concept—
that I am a God of love—that fear has no place
in me—you will have a powerful tool for determining whether or not any particular words speak
my truth.

Only Versus Love

Consider the sentences that form the pillars
of your belief system:

"Whoever believes in him is not condemned."
"No one comes to the Father except
through me."

Those two sentences are fused into one master belief:

Only through Jesus Christ can you be saved.

Do you believe both these statements to be perfectly true:

"Only through Jesus Christ can you be saved."
"God loves you."

You've been taught that "only through Jesus" is the single belief you need to have about being saved. It has taught you that this belief and my love are one and the same.

When you say the words, "Only through Jesus Christ can you be saved," does any fear come up? Are you certain or uncertain? Does the question of certainty bring up fear?

Ask yourself, "What if Jesus is not the only way?" Or, "What will happen if I don't accept Jesus as my Savior?" Do either of those questions elicit fear in you?

What about the statement, "God loves you"? Is it possible to summon fear when you hear those words?

Remember, you will feel me through love. Something is amiss if you feel fear.

Do you believe that I love you unconditionally? If so, how does that impact the significance of the

word "only" in the statement, "Only through
Jesus Christ can you be saved"?

My love for you is not dependent on what
you do or do not know. I would not condemn my
children for not knowing something any more than
you would condemn your children for not knowing
algebra in kindergarten.

Whether or not Jesus is the only way, I could
never condemn you for not knowing that truth or
not understanding it, because my doing that
would interfere with your ability to determine
whether or not it is true. You can be scared into
believing something called the truth, but you can't
be scared into knowing it is the truth. Why would
I envelop the truth in so much fear that you could
never reach it, leaving you no choice but to blindly
accept it?

The truth waits eternally for you to find it,
just as I do. My truth is love. My words are light.
If you seek and find the truth while on the earth,
your life will progress in grandeur. If you choose
to never seek, however, you will not be judged,
though you may experience a life that is unfulfilled
in certain ways. If you don't seek the truth, you
will be condemned to not know the truth—that's
all—and the truth is grand.

The spiritual teachings of Jesus, and the love
he manifested in the world, are there for your benefit—nothing else. There is no divine rod coming
down in absolute judgment, deciding if your soul

is saved or damned based on your acceptance or rejection of those teachings. There is no punishment associated with your relationship to me or to Jesus.

If you believe Jesus is my son, and you know I am love, then Jesus is love. You know in your heart that love is the domain of his teachings. Anything you are told that falls outside the domain of love—such as you will suffer eternal physical torment if you don't know or believe something—is the stuff of ego and the ignorance of men (their ignor-ance of love), who could only understand his teachings in the most literal terms.

If you must find God, and "there is only one way to find God," then that is a command. It leaves you no options. If you try any other way, you will not find God. If you believe that, you are likely to be afraid, and fear has no place in love.

But the fear of not finding God is nothing compared to the fear of what will happen to you in the afterlife if you don't hold the right beliefs. You've been told that if you don't believe in the one and only Son, Jesus, you won't be saved.

What does it mean to be saved? According to what you've been told, being saved means that your soul will go to heaven after you die—you'll be saved from going to hell. What could be more terrifying than eternity in hell?

Regardless of whether "only through Jesus" is right or wrong, please understand that I do not work through mechanisms of fear.

It might be argued that "only through Jesus" is a loving message because it is telling souls something they need to know. But if the reason for the statement is based on love, why would any aspect of it elicit fear? The message could just as easily be delivered in a way that does not create fear: "Through Jesus Christ you can be saved," or, "Through Jesus Christ you can find God." Inserting the word "only" transforms either sentence into a fearful proposition.

For ages, hell has been used as leverage to get you to believe. Surely there are better reasons than avoiding hell to seek God or Jesus. Is fear required in order to love God?

When you consider the Jesus you know in your heart, instead of the details of your beliefs in your head, do you believe he intended your spirituality to be governed by fear? Do you believe that the sum total of the Gospel he delivered was to teach you that by accepting him as the Lord you would be spared from hell and go to heaven?

Surely there are better reasons than going to heaven to seek God or Jesus.

The life, spirit, and lessons of Jesus can only be understood through your own seeking. They may be taught, told, or shown to your mind, ears, and eyes, but are learned only by your soul.

Seeking is driven by love, not fear. Love is the way to the kingdom of heaven, and you know it. I designed you to know it. Trust your heart—more.

The Lockbox of Fear

When you take the word "only" out of this sentence and say, "Through Jesus Christ you can find God," you do not diminish the truth or take away from the divinity of Jesus Christ. Then why does the word "only" need to be there?

Only *through* Jesus has been misinterpreted to mean only Jesus: only Jesus knew me personally; the closest you can get to me or Jesus is to worship us; you can stop looking for me once you learn that Jesus is the Lord and accept him as your Savior.

Finding God is what's important. Stressing the word "only" serves to ensure your worship of Jesus Christ as your Lord, while Jesus' wish for you to find God and evolve spiritually is too often ignored.

Remember: The words of Jesus are intended to bring you to God and the kingdom, *not to Jesus*.

He speaks often of his Father in heaven so that you may know the Father. He speaks of your finding the kingdom yourself. He guides you to find God through him. Not once, however, does Jesus tell you to seek *him*. Yet this is what you've been told to do.

In the centuries following Jesus' death, there were great conflicts surrounding the question of whether Jesus was equal to God or made by God. Your belief system is an offspring of a determination made ages ago that Jesus and God were one and the same. The differentiation between God and Jesus was swept away; the humanity of Jesus got taken away, as if to acknowledge his humanity would diminish his divinity.

Rather than bringing you closer to me, your religion became a system to perpetrate your separation: God is God, Jesus is Jesus, you are only you, and this is how God designed it. However, being lowly, sinful, and separated is just fine, because after you die you will be forgiven and dwell in Paradise for all eternity as a result of your belief in who you were told Jesus is. This ideology has only increased the distance between us and caused you to believe that the love you feel for me, and the prayers you say to me, are the extent to which you can have relationship with me, at least for now.

The egos of those who founded your belief system, over the course of a few centuries after Jesus died, couldn't be humble enough to acknowledge truth that it was their creation—their response to an awareness of God—because that would allow for the possibility of error, in which case the system itself might be called into question and their ego's security would be in jeopardy.

So they called your belief system perfect—the creation of God. And to protect it (and themselves) even more, they further declared that to question it or look outside the belief system for answers could condemn you to hell. Any doubts or questions you might have were deemed temptations of the devil.

Which seems more of a devil to you: the force that presents you with a God and a belief system you can never question, or the force that invites you to question and seek the truth of God for yourself?

Only love can give you the right answer. Jesus preached and practiced for you to do the latter.

Not being allowed to question grants your ego exactly what it desires—security in separation. Your ego knows that if you are fixated on the divinity of Jesus as God's one and only Son, you will not be looking beyond what you've been taught about him, because you could never aspire to be like Jesus or to know what he knew anyway.

Unfortunately, while the ego's position is secured, your soul is secured in a different way. "Only" [through Jesus] traps you in one specific belief. It is a lockbox of limitation for your soul. The lockbox keeps the truth inside it and your seeking mind locked out. It's a man-made device that uses the fear of condemnation to protect your ego by preventing you from asking questions. You've been told what is the "only" way, so you

don't have to think, or seek, or find. Simply accept
it or not; be saved or perish.

"Why is this truth so?" you ask your father.
"Because I said so—that's why," he replies.

The founders of your belief system came up
with their fixed set of beliefs concerning Jesus,
locked them in the box, and called them the
holy words—not to be questioned—for all time.
Paradoxically, if you open the box to examine
the contents, you're in faithless violation; if you
accept without question what you've been told
is the truth, you can never *know* the contents.
Seek by questioning the truth of the words "only
through Jesus" and you are condemned for your
lack of faith; accept the truth blindly and you
never get to find out if it's true. Just keep the
sacred lockbox on a pedestal, you're told, and
have faith that by doing so you will be saved
when the time comes.
I invite you, in love-filled anticipation, to
question me, and to grow and learn from me.
You naturally have questions and maybe some
doubts. This is honest. Yet you allow yourself to
believe that uncertainty, curiosity, and an open
mind are gateways to hell, and thus, you believe
that honesty is damnation. Isn't that silly? Do
you believe I could ever condemn you for being
honest? Would I, the loving God you believe in,

cast you into hell because heaven forbids you to harbor any doubts?

You believe Jesus spoke the words "seek and you shall find," and you believe they are my words, but do you seek? Or do you simply accept what you've been taught to believe and not trouble yourself to seek?

Your ego knows you well. It knows what tools are at its disposal. Everything surrounding the word "God" is draped in holiness. Being caught up in worship keeps you from seeking, and then you are not doing what Jesus preached for you to do.

Not thinking or questioning may be your religion's commandments but they are not mine. You are told to believe in the Gospels, but nowhere in the Gospels are you told to blindly believe everything others tell you is the truth. There's a critical difference between the words of scripture and the interpretation of those words. Just because the Gospel exists doesn't mean the way others have interpreted it is the Gospel too. And even if they have interpreted all the words correctly, you still need to come to understanding them on your own if you are to benefit from them.

The only value of blind faith is that if you allow yourself to believe in something, you might then be inspired to gain further spiritual understanding. If your faith entails a dark side born of what will happen to you if you don't believe, fear must be your copilot. Faith marred by fear thwarts your path forward. You will be tense, close-minded, and apprehensive about learning truth for yourself, because your religion commands you to accept its truth as my own.

Blind Faith

Blind faith, you have been told, is of divine value. This rule works well for the separate being who is seeking comfort in being separate because it provides the only answer you'll ever need and prevents you from the discomfort of asking questions to which you don't know the answers.

Blind faith, in and of itself, holds no value and earns nothing for your soul. The only value it has is your belief in me, which can and should inspire you to seek me, and keep on finding me.

The blind faith you've been prescribed is harmful because it tells you that you will gain entrance to heaven where you'll be with me after you die and often causes you to not see the potential of your relationship with me right now—on the earth. It tells you that you can't find answers for yourself, answers that might transform you.

Will believing in Jesus decide the fate of your soul? Have you sought this answer from Jesus? He left plenty of material behind for you to study.

Have you examined his words? You have the ability to find the answer for yourself. You don't have to merely accept what you are told.

I gave you a great tool for progressing spiritually and evolving as a being—your mind. Blind faith tells you that you need not rely on your mind to answer the bigger questions or determine higher truths because Jesus did all the work for you. How convenient. Your religion, which was created after Jesus died, wanted you to accept all the answers it gave as coming from Jesus. It declared them by self-appointed divine authority. It warned you of grave peril for your soul should you think too much and corrupt the integrity of your faith.

I gave you your mind not so you should fear it but so you'd use it to help you. What kind of God do you take me for, that I would give you the gift and power to think and then condemn you for doing so?

This fear, according to his words, is not what Jesus wanted for you. He wanted you to come to know God personally—to engage your mind in order to find answers. Why would Jesus implore you to ask if he had already given you all the answers? Why seek, if the answers are already found? You are taught that Jesus is the ultimate role model, but then you are told to ignore some of what he said.

He taught you to love and believe and not to

fear. He taught you that the kingdom of God is yours to find, and that you could find it on your own. Jesus advocated a genuine relationship with God over any religious practice that would simply go through the motions, or impede people's path to finding God, or adversely affect their well-being.

Now, two thousand years later, the tables have turned, and once again an old guard of bold people have declared what you ought to believe based on their own ego-driven beliefs—our way or no way, believe or else.

Beware these heralds of fear, gloom, and doom. Lost are the ones who believe that I command in absolutes. They are dragging you down to *their* self-created misery. It is they who fear their own lack of certainty—their own lack of firsthand knowledge.

They are afraid to think for themselves because they fear me. While they profess me to be a merciful God of love, privately they believe I am an unyielding, jealous, and judgmental God who will cast them out as faithless for having the temerity to think. Why? Because this is what they too were taught throughout their lives, and what they now, in turn, teach to you, often with the best of intentions.

It's humorous because they are aware of their limitations, and yet they are still sure they know the answers when it comes to God, creation, and death.

It's sad because if you believe that only Jesus

could know me personally (only he was my son), and the best you can do is to worship Jesus in order to reach me after you die, you transform yourself from a beautiful being of unlimited potential into one prone to a lifetime of limitation.

Jesus taught you to follow in his footsteps; he taught that you could achieve what he achieved. Yet you've been taught that your only spiritual goal should be to accept the truth of Jesus Christ as your Lord and Savior.

Truth

What is truth? Men have fought and killed each other for thousands of years because they disagreed on what the truth is—who God is, what God is called, what system of belief is right, and which others are therefore wrong. It's like fighting over what love is—no fight is more foolish, more futile, or more tragic.

Many with absolute faith believe that Jesus spoke the truth with divine authority when he stated, "No one comes to the Father except through me." Belief, however, is different from fact; even one with absolute faith can't state for certain that Jesus said those words at all, and accepting that he did say them, can't state for certain what they mean. One can only state what one believes the words mean. These truths need not undermine faith.

The authority of the words "only through Jesus," and what they mean, has been passed down through the generations and to you today. And keepers of that authority believe they are commanded by me to accept those words as what they understand them to mean. Then they say these are God's words, rather than say they *believe* these are God's words. Their meaning of the words is defined as God's truth, and you are commanded to accept it.

Remember: I am not commanding you to accept *any* truth.

I present to you the truth. You may perceive the truth that sits before you or you may feel something to be true. However, there is no sentence presented to you that you can know is the truth before going through the internal process of mind that brings you to that truth.

You cannot be commanded to know the truth. If you are, it's never actually the truth you accept. It's only an image of something called the truth.

When you were younger and learned your multiplication tables, you could memorize all the answers and be able to recite them at any time. For example, two times two equals four. But only when you process what that means, and realize if you lay down two sticks, then two more next to them, two sticks two times gives you four sticks, do you truly understand multiplication.

Likewise, you could memorize every word that Jesus said in the Bible, but spiritual truth is what you come to know through your own mind and heart—through me—and this knowledge transforms you. Your search for this truth is your own path, and your path should be one of inspiring revelations, not conflict. Your spirituality is not supposed to take you to a dark, frightening place with terrible consequences for your soul.

I love you so. I wish you knew the unconditional nature of that love. The tyranny of fear that is draped over your soul is absurd. It's absurd to know I love you and yet believe I would condemn you to eternal torment if you didn't happen to believe the right beliefs.

For many people, belief is based on whatever religion they happen to have been born into. Do you suppose my love is reserved only for those who happened to be raised in a Christian home? What about those who never heard of Jesus Christ? Do you truly believe I condemn them to hell based on the circumstance of their life? Do you think if you were raised in a Muslim home, in a Muslim land, you would hold the same beliefs you do now?

Salvation of the soul is too often devolved into the basic matter of whether you will go to heaven or hell after you die. Why worry about the details of an afterlife, which are beyond your comprehension? Even the Bible does not give details concerning what happens when you die.

You don't have to pretend to understand that which you do not; you need only be genuine. There are many answers you can't know while on the earth; humility need not be contrived. It occurs naturally as a result of learning the truth, which is that you know so close to nothing, it can be said you know nothing at all.

The most difficult questions you can ask have been, and still are, unanswerable for you.

Was humanity created on purpose? Who or what is God?

Your ego deludes you into believing you have the answers. It deludes you into believing you need to know those answers. Its job is to make you feel secure in order to make itself secure.

Will believing in Jesus decide the fate of your soul?

Must your belief supersede your desire to seek such answers yourself?

Remember: I do not tell you *this* or *that* is *the* truth. It is you who decides what the truth is. Don't let anyone tell you what the truth is. Don't let anyone tell you what God's words are. Let words be spoken or displayed to you but seek within yourself to determine their validity.

Do you think Jesus has an ego requiring you to declare your blind allegiance to him alone, cutting off all other paths of learning?

[*But it's written,* I finally replied.]

It is Written

Pang goes the fear again, eh? How you have loved absolute statements like, "It's written." These words have granted you everlasting security. No more thinking. No more seeking. Just peace and comfort in the written words of God, answering all questions, laying down all laws.

What does "It is written" mean? It is written in the Bible—the one and only text you have to ultimately guide your life, you're told. It is often taught that I wrote every word in the Bible. But such an absolute statement is yet another manifestation of the paradox we've been discussing. You can't question the words of God, which means you can't determine for yourself if they are true. The lockbox is not open for discussion. However, if you allow your belief system to dictate what is God's truth, instead of finding it for yourself, you're at risk of the belief system becoming the steward of your soul, rather than God.

Those who created your belief system and those who have kept it have you so caught up in the absolute notion that its words are God's words, you are prevented from looking into the origins of those words. With ultimate fear on the one hand

and God's love on the other, they have kept you in spiritual subservience, even while there has been good intention to lovingly serve you.

I tell you, however, there is an endless amount to be learned from studying the history of the Bible's words, as well as from discovering for yourself what those words mean independent of that history. How ironic that I should welcome your open mind with love as the path to finding me, while these others, claiming to shepherd your soul in my name, preach that you should deny your open mind because it will lead you away from me. They have converted your spirituality into a win or lose scenario.

The truth being kept from you is that you don't need to subscribe to their two-choice paradigm. If you are busy worrying about whether you will go to heaven or hell—the only two options presented to you—you may fail to understand that it was those who created your belief system, not I, who have put that choice to you.

Accept their win or lose scenario and you are caught in their paradox—you can't seek because you have to blindly believe; but if you blindly believe you can't get to know me. Your soul is captured. The more of you captured, the safer *they* are. The more believers in their ideology there are, the more validated are their beliefs.

It is written: "No one comes to the Father except through me."

Did I write that sentence? As they tell it, Jesus said this as me incarnate, and it is written in my book, so they are my words.

The authority of the Bible as a whole, and the meaning of the words therein, must remain stuff of belief and cannot be called fact. That does not detract from the authority of my words; it means there is too much about the ancient past you can never know. Even if all the words were indeed perfect, you could never know that, you could only believe it.

Is "only through me" a true statement? Is every statement in the Bible true? Is every word in the Bible written by God?

The words in the Bible, in and of themselves, hold no spiritual meaning. All meaning lies in what you ascribe to them.

These are good questions. They can lead to knowledge.

The answers do not matter. They do not affect the value of the written words.

Your Bible has messages of truth and wisdom for you to find. But the value of those messages is to be found in the words themselves, regardless of who wrote them, even if you believe that author to be me.

Words are just words. Knowing who wrote or said the words doesn't change their meaning for better or worse. If someone unknown had said the words, "Love your enemies," would that diminish their value?

For too long my name has been used to keep people from having to actually understand the words they so vehemently defend. "God spoke—accept and obey" is the creed of too many religions. Caught up in the argument over which words are God's, you are tempted to forget the primary importance of coming to understand the words themselves. If you truly believe all the words in your Bible are mine, shouldn't you then have the desire to study them earnestly?

Why must it be an all or nothing choice? Why do you have to believe God wrote every word in your Bible or none of them? How you should regard the Bible in terms of Godly content is not a matter beyond your comprehension.

My words are in your Bible. If you continue to seek, you will come to know which ones they are. Man's words are also in the Bible. All you need to know is that any human being had a hand in writing your Bible—even if only as an inspired scribe—to know that it likely contains flaws. Anything written with human hands warrants examination—not blind acceptance.

If you heard Jesus speak, you could accept his Gospel directly. But the fact is, men were responsible for getting that Gospel to you. They were inspired, yes, but the Gospels you read are successive iterations, branched from the original source.

No one on earth can state with certainty exactly what words Jesus said and what their precise meaning was in every case. Even the closest translations can still miss the nuances or subtleties of the original language. That is why the meaning you glean from the words is more important than the words themselves. The words are not holy. Only your interpretation of them can be.

You were told "only through Jesus;" told that the Bible is my book; told that all of its words are mine; told that if you question any of the words or their validity, you are lacking in faith. If you're lacking in faith, you're told, it's a short step to damnation. Damned if you open the box; in the dark if you don't.

If I love you, how could I damn you?

I damn you because I love you? It would be silly if so many people didn't believe it. The truth is yours to decide. It's yours to seek and find. You decide which words are mine.

You will not be saved solely because of one belief you hold. Nor will you be condemned solely because of one belief you did not hold. You will not be saved because you know one or more particular truths; nor will you be condemned because you did not know. You will not be saved because you believed blindly that I wrote every word in the Bible. You will not be damned because you didn't.

Please now, stop.

Take a deep breath.

Know this, remember this:

You Are Already Saved

CHAPTER 16
SALVATION

Get on with the love. Get on with the seeking.

According to what I'd been taught, my soul is in danger; I need Jesus Christ to save me from hell and grant me eternal life in heaven. The words of Jesus, however, offer us a far richer and more profound meaning.

If needing to be saved means your soul is lacking something fundamental that it requires for salvation, you are already saved. If being saved means simply being spared from a fiery place called hell, you are already saved. You may be so caught up in the fear of what to do or believe in order to be saved, it doesn't occur to you that you don't need to be saved in these ways.

A few thousand years ago, you might have believed that if you got in a boat and sailed to the horizon, you would fall off the edge of the world, and this would have been a normal belief. If you were condemned and put on a boat to sail straight to your death, chances are that when you were far enough from shore to not be seen, you would have dived off the boat and swam for your life. You'd do anything to save yourself. You'd rather take your chances with the sharks than sail off the edge of the world. Fear would prevent you from realizing there might be another possibility: there is no edge of the world.

It's the same with the belief that your soul needs to be saved from going to a fiery hell after you die—that life on earth is a believe-or-burn ultimatum of extremes and the meaning of your spiritual life is nothing more than accepting Jesus Christ as your Savior in order to get to heaven. This fearful belief system began in ancient times, over the centuries following Jesus' death. It doesn't mean you have to keep believing it today.

You are a beautiful soul who already has everything you need for salvation. Don't let anyone tell you otherwise. If you believe you are incomplete or not good enough, you will fear that you won't be able to acquire what you need to be complete. How much greater then is the fear that you will not acquire what you need to get to heaven? The love offered through Jesus and his teachings can guide you to salvation. There is no threat involved.

Do not ignore the hell that comes to mind and how it makes you feel when you imagine the afterlife consequences of not being saved. Your faith in Jesus Christ does not demand that you accept all the beliefs men have linked to his name. Whether their reasons for threatening you with hell were based on a desire for control or on the most loving intention to save you, in your accepting the ancient belief that you need to be saved, you are left in fear. If you need to be saved from something, there is something to fear.

Once again, we have a major problem resulting from the limitations of our vocabulary and our need to reduce profound spiritual understandings to either/or absolutes. What we just discussed is the traditional, literal understanding of "saved." In these next few chapters, we will explore a far more expansive—and, in fact, more glorious—understanding of being saved (salvation). We've lived under fear since the first centuries of Christianity, presuming that if we were not saved we would be damned. It's the best we could do in ancient times when we first began trying to understand the teachings of Jesus, and we've held onto it ever since because we've been afraid to question certain beliefs we've linked to God. To this day, untold millions of us believe that God uses the fear of hell as a means to drive us to Jesus.

Are we ready to gently let go of the thought that God uses fear as a way to bring us to his love or to Jesus? For so many of us—even the most religious of us—it just seems too good to be true that fear has no place in love, and that God loves us absolutely *no matter what*.

<hr />

Do you believe Christ is love? Proceeding from this belief, the words of Jesus are there for your illumination, not to make you afraid. His words are *good* seed, not seeds of fear. He preached a ministry of love and your limitless capability to know God. Jesus had a greater agenda than simply saving you for the next round. And while he preached for you to believe in him, that didn't mean you were inherently lacking as a human being.

When Jesus says, "The kingdom of heaven is like treasure hidden in a field,"[1] does he follow that with, "but you don't have what it takes to find it"? When he says, "Ask and it will be given to you; seek and you will find," does he say that you are not fully equipped to follow this teaching?

If you were missing something you needed in order to find the kingdom of God, it would have been terribly remiss of Jesus not to tell you that. Instead, he says you must come to the kingdom as a child, not as an adult who knows all the answers, or you will never enter.[2]

If Christ is love, then the pursuit of spiritual understanding and growth in his name should be about nothing but love. In love, there is no room or reason for you to fear that the details of your belief may not be exactly right, or to worry about whether your understandings of scripture are correct. God wants you to learn and grow spiritually. Do you really imagine that your Creator, who knows your imperfections, makes a final judgment of you based on your knowledge or belief while you are still on your path to finding the answers? Or that you, in your imperfection, could do something wrong that God would never forgive?

Accept that you are loved unconditionally—not as some nice saying, but truly. Next time you look at yourself in the mirror of judgment, imagine you have a seven-year-old child who spilled a glass of milk. Would that cause you to declare you will never forgive them? Can you imagine your child doing anything that would cause you to withdraw your love? On the contrary, you would no doubt take on the world to

---

1 Matthew 13:44.
2 See Matthew 18:3; Mark 10:15; Luke 18:17.

defend their innocence, maybe even in light of a true crime. Do you imagine God loves you less?

The Forgiveness of Sin

Some of the words in our lexicon of spirituality have, over the ages, gathered negative connotations. One of these is "sin." Many of us have been told that belief in Jesus Christ is the most important criterion for salvation, but, at the same time, have had sin evoked as a barrier to being saved. Such a serious word sin is—laden with judgment—drenched in religious significance. We've heard throughout our life that Jesus died for our sins. It doesn't get more serious than that. To view sin only in these terms can cast dark clouds over our perception of God's love, and it can allow us to miss the practical understanding of sin that would benefit our life.

As we discussed back in chapter 10, sin is usually taken literally to mean a wrongful act—something we do to harm ourselves or others. The harm could be minor and easily fixed, or deeply scarring and doing permanent damage. We then go a step further to say that sin is a transgression against God for which we are judged. However, we also discussed a spiritual definition of sin underlying the literal. In a spiritual sense, death is the state of separation from God and sin is the act that puts us there. Put another way, sin is anything that separates us from our highest self.

Let's say, for example, we choose to drink a lot of alcohol on a daily basis. We are then choosing to live a somewhat blurred existence. While it may not be impossible to find God (or simply to live in harmony with our idea of righteousness), our mind and emotions, which act as our guides, will be impaired. Drinking becomes a sin when we are no longer able to find God. Or, we could just say drinking becomes a sin when we are no longer able to live the life we want and be happy. We are also damaging our body, which can have its own repercussions (separation from good health). Or maybe our drinking leads to others in our life being hurt. Understanding why our actions (or inactions) led to any kind of suffering can make sin, on its own, a great practical teacher.

Adding God's judgment doesn't give us the same kind of constructive feedback. Perhaps we will do the right thing because we feel we have to, but if the reason why we do it is not personally tangible enough, chances are the change won't last. The purest reason to change sinful behavior is to benefit ourself and therefore others. And isn't that doing it for God, anyway—being the best person we can be?

Perhaps you'd agree, however, that drinking too much, even with all the harm that may result, is a relatively minor sin, because we can still make a better choice, change our actions, and fix our situation. But what about the more damaging, egregious sins?

Leaving aside issues such as murder or sexual assault, let's say someone cheats on their spouse. Perhaps their marriage ends and the lives of both people, as well as their children (if they have any), are adversely affected in long term, important ways. Or what if while driving, someone looks down at their phone when a message comes in and causes an accident that kills someone. In such a situation, the damage can never be reversed—someone lost their life, and there is also the collateral damage to all the loved ones connected to both parties.

If we look at just the sinner in these cases, the outcomes resulting from their actions might create all manner of psychological trauma and suffering (unless, of course, they are a psychopath who doesn't care). However, in one sense, the results of major sins are the same as those of minor ones: existing in the state of being cut off from God or from our best selves—that is, spiritual death. In these cases, however, that state might seem exponentially harder to get out of due to the irreversibility of the outcomes. Nonetheless, it is at any point of feeling disconnected due to our own actions that we may most fear losing God's love.[1]

The question is whether the state of spiritual death is actually dictated by God, or whether it is something we create for ourselves. We do enough damage to ourselves through sin without bringing Godly judgment into the equation. We might feel emotional pain, regret, remorse, or guilt as a result of sinful actions, or we might have psychological battles to face, but these can also be valuable indicators of right and wrong, or of what is good or bad for ourselves and others.

Whatever sins or causes we could ever have, the deeper suffering occurs in our soul when we choose to believe that God's love is withdrawn from us. Or, put another way, we choose to believe we don't deserve love—we don't deserve to feel good or be happy, and then we are in darkness. That kind of spiraling self-torture can go on indefinitely as pain begets the pain of being in pain, and so on.

---

1 This is just one particular way to express this, of course. In nonspiritual terms, one who does something morally wrong or reckless that causes irreversible harm to oneself or others might incur the same kind of trauma, fear, or feeling lost.

In my experience, the more clarity I've had, or the closer I am to God, the more painful it's been when I blow it, lose that clarity, and simply can't find God in the darkness—I can't find my highest thinking and best self. Or when, because of life circumstances or relationships gone wrong, I became depressed, I wondered if I'd ever be truly happy again. But any time I've ever felt those ways, through perseverance and my desire to overcome (and sometimes, I believe, with the guidance of Spirit) I was able to retrace my steps, find out where I went wrong, and figure out what I could have done more wisely. In doing so, I learned that my suffering was self-inflicted, not a punishment from God, and the suffering then became a great teacher, letting me know how to avoid repeating my mistake.

It's usually when we get to such a low, and we are deeply sad, angry, lost, or exhausted, that we look up and beseech God, "Where are you?" At such times we are in essence asking God, "Why have you forsaken me?" And we find God staring back, saying, "Why have *you* forsaken *me*?"

God's love is never withdrawn.

Rather it is we who choose to pull away from the consciousness of God, or, said another way, from our clarity. It is we who can choose what to think, and that choice is one of the few things in life we can control. We can then redirect our thoughts and take different actions; we can change our ways (repent). As for Godly judgment or condemnation, if you still want to hold onto those literal biblical understandings, you've certainly read enough now to know the Bible's possible timing for that judgment. God's love, however, is shown by the Bible's more immediate solution to the problem of sin.

At times in the Gospels, when Jesus heals people, he says, "Your sins are forgiven." The word "sins," in this context, refers to the totality of our perceived separation from God. Although physical illness may have a physical cause, the perceived separation from God (spiritual death) is a metaphysical impediment to his ultimate healing force.[1]

Separation from God is how Jesus perceived sickness; this is what sickness was, relative to the fully realized spirit of Jesus. When he took the hand of the mortally ill and said, "Rise now," he infused them with the light of his truth, as if he were saying: *There is nothing here but my divine presence; awaken to the truth of it within you and be separate from God no more; the perceived separation of sickness cannot exist in you.* Their sins were forgiven—wiped away like a debt would be forgiven—clearing the way for them to rise out of spiritual death, cleansed and reborn in the light of God.

Isn't this concept supposed to have applied to all the world in the sacrifice of his life? If Jesus died to pay for the sins of the world, then the sins of the world—past, present, and future—were forgiven. So, are your sins forgiven or aren't they? It can't be both. Even though you may believe you could transgress against God and thereby incur his wrath, if what it

---

1 One last restating: God is a word—a term for expression. You could as well say, "The perceived separation from Spirit is an impediment to its ultimate healing force." The same truths can be expressed in different language. Invoking one's will, coupled with health and life-style changes, are as much "finding God" and allowing healing forces to flow, as concerns healing. The message is all that counts; the names, words, language, or context are not sacrosanct ever.

says in the Bible is true, you are already forgiven. Of course there is an obvious catch there: You must accept Jesus Christ as your Lord in order to receive the forgiveness. But does that make logical sense?

Let's accept as true that the sins of the world were forgiven through Jesus Christ. If the world were that mortally ill person, then Jesus infused it with the light of his truth. The world has been shown that the darkness of separation is an illusion. Do you believe Jesus' forgiveness requires your faith in order to be activated? Is the world actually dark until you believe it is light?

If Jesus did what he is said to have done, the world was left in a state of forgiveness, a state of grace, a state of love. Sin is turning away from that state. You may have been taught you were born a sinner and, as you inevitably act according to your nature, you must ask for forgiveness in order to regain God's grace. Now, instead of viewing yourself as a sinner, consider that you are a beautiful soul—a child of God—who occasionally acts against your nature and sins. Rather than reaching down from heaven and pardoning you because you have asked, God would only remind you of the eternal state of forgiveness you live in. In that reminder, your Father says, "Now sin no more."

When you choose love, you are deciding you don't want to live in separation from God any longer and you recognize that your sins are already forgiven. You don't want to harm yourself or others, and you forgive yourself for the temporary ignorance that caused you to think or behave in separate ways.

This is one understanding of salvation—as the forgiveness of sin. It is the understanding that God loves you unconditionally. It doesn't mean it's okay to sin. It doesn't mean the wicked do not need to face real-world justice or repent and undergo a spiritual reckoning for their own well-being or for others'. It doesn't mean any of us shouldn't acknowledge any wrong we've done or mistakes we've made and change for the better. It means that no matter what you do, you are loved, and the slate is clean. God's arms are always open to welcome you. God's forgiveness is eternal.

This is precisely what is meant by, "You are already saved."

Being Saved

> For God did not send his Son into the world
> to condemn the world, but to save the world
> through him. (John 3:17)

> For I did not come to judge the world, but to
> save the world. (John 12:47)

Accordingly, Jesus has been called the Savior of humanity. What did Jesus mean by, "I came to save the world"? Did he finish the job? Are you saved?

Many of us have been taught that we are not born saved. There is still something missing. Perhaps being baptized as a baby gives you that something. Or perhaps it is when you make a mature, conscious decision to accept God as central in your life. Most believers, however, would probably agree that you are the missing link in Jesus' completion of the job. You must accept him as your Savior in order to be saved.

This understanding of salvation comes from the perspective of separation. It tells you that you are separate from God, but then tells you how you can be with him someday. This perspective first creates your need to be saved and then tells you what to believe in order to be saved.

As it is written in another one of the most quoted verses from the Gospel of John:

> For God so loved the world that he gave his one
> and only Son, that whoever believes in him shall
> not perish but have eternal life. (John 3:16)

Now let's look again at the verse that follows this:

> For God did not send his Son into the world
> to condemn the world, but to save the world
> through him. (John 3:17)

John 3:16 seems to say what most of our denominations teach: believe in Jesus in order to be saved. John 3:17, however, says Jesus came to save the world, not condemn it. There seems to be a contradiction here between what these verses say and what is commonly taught, which is that Jesus sacrificed himself in order to save the world. If you are told the work of Jesus cannot be completed until you choose to believe, doesn't that mean Jesus did not finish his job of saving the world?

The resolution has been to say that Jesus did his job and left you with a choice to believe in him or not—you *might* be saved. Jesus is the Redeemer, but you must believe in him to be redeemed. Stop and think about whether these two ideas make sense together (Jesus saved the world; you must believe). If you feel confused, it can be tempting to just accept what you were told to believe and not think about it too much. But wouldn't you agree that God does not want you to settle for confusion? God wants your clarity and understanding.

The only way to truly resolve the seeming contradiction between these two ideas is to understand that you are already saved. With this understanding, you don't have to believe in order for salvation to happen. Rather, salvation already is and you believe in it—if, that is, you believe Jesus did what he came here to do ("For I did not come to judge the world, but to save the world").

Why would you not believe that Jesus finished his work? Did he not say, "It is finished"?[1]

Saying the world is already saved is another way of saying that the sins of the world were forgiven. It is another way of stating that Jesus Christ came into the world and died in order that people should have spiritual life. It's not that Jesus died to save you; he died for you to know that you are saved. He did not come to bring the light to you; he came to inform you that you are the light.

God and his light already are and always have been, and the truth is that his light is inside you—it is you, whether you believe it or not. That light, in and of itself, is your already saved self. And yet, that doesn't mean there isn't work to do

---

1 John 19:30.

in order for you to fulfill your highest potential, or to have a balanced, peaceful, and happy life.

The completion of Jesus' mission does not depend on your believing in him. Jesus would not be very powerful if he required your belief to empower him. Rather, he is empowered already, and you choose to believe it. You are already saved, and you choose to believe it.

You might then ask, "Why do I (or anyone) need to believe if I am already saved?"

Being already saved means that God is real, which, in turn, begs the question: "If God is real, why do you need to believe in God?"

You need to believe in God in order to know God. God *is,* whether you believe in God or not, but you can live your entire life without ever finding God. Likewise, you need to believe in the Son in order to know the Son—to be alive in Spirit. As if he'd said: *Believe, and therefore seek; believe, and therefore love others.* But he didn't mean: *Believe in me and stop there.* You believe in the Son, in order to come to know spiritual truth for yourself.

This does not mean, however, that unless you believe, there is no salvation. Salvation does not go away. If someone doesn't believe in God, does that mean God goes away? You are saved whether you believe it or not; you might not, however, be participating in a relationship with God. You can choose to live in light or darkness, but as long as you exist, your soul is not at risk, ever, of being permanently cut off from God.

It could seem that already being saved is not news if we were already saved by believing in Jesus. But we may also have been taught that this saving comes only after we die, as we enter heaven. Holding that view can deprive us of the desire for the full measure of spiritual wealth available to us while we're alive.

If "believe in me and get to heaven" were the only message Jesus came here to deliver, the Gospels would have been four very short books. Or it would mean that the Gospels are just four hefty books of rhetoric and sayings that don't really matter enough for us to read. The divinity of Jesus is not to be slighted, but neither should the full range of his teachings and ministry.

There is a greater spiritual purpose to our being here than knowing God's name and where we will go when we die. Jesus invited us to believe in and seek God because he knew we would find God if we did. He knew from firsthand experience that we would find more knowledge of Spirit with each passing day—with each passing hour—commensurate with the energy and faith we put into our seeking.

What we find is ours to keep. The treasures of eternal salvation are gained through the seeking we do on earth. Would you like to leave this earth with nothing more than you had when you arrived? Or would you like to leave with trunkfuls of treasure? Will you choose to be saved only after you die, or will you be saved while you live?

Despite the great faith you have in God, you might be

surprised to learn how much thought you put into keeping him at a distance. There is much more than religious faith surrounding the belief that you will be awarded salvation only when you die; there is purpose behind it, driven by the ego.

CHAPTER 17

THE RECONCILIATION OF EGO AND GOD

It can be frightening to confront ideas that conflict with our beliefs. For most of our life, any questions pertaining to God and what to believe may have been answered for us by others, leaving the great mystery of God of no concern to unravel while we are alive, because we have all the answers we need for this life.

Consciously or unconsciously, having those answers is a great comfort. To entertain new ideas that conflict with those answers threatens that sense of comfort. We will either accept the new ideas and brave the unknown or deny their validity. If we were raised to believe xyz or else go to hell, and then someone comes along and says, "Here is abc, instead of xyz," we're probably not going to accept it. We might believe this is a simple matter of rejecting the new ideas, but there is more to it than that.

Words are just words. Ideas are just ideas. The only meaning they have is what we give them. Therefore, if hearing new ideas causes us to feel angry, offended, or frustrated, something deep within us is generating those feelings. To suddenly question what we know or believe can cause us to be spiritually afraid. Not only is much of what we thought for a lifetime called into question, but in that moment it can feel as if we've lost God, which in turn may cause us to worry about our salvation—whether we are still in good standing with God.

Ideas like being already saved, or of it not mattering (in a soul-threatening way) whether or not God wrote every word in the Bible, or that it's possible for you to know God while alive, may open new doors of knowledge, but they also may go against everything you've believed to be true about God for your entire life. Entertaining new ideas at this point may simply not be worth the risk or the pain. You could feel exposed, vulnerable, and alone in very foreign territory—why volunteer for that?

Do these feelings sound familiar by now? What is the part of you that responds from and adheres to a paradigm of separation? It's your ego.

As a separate being, your ego is constantly trying to protect itself in the guise of protecting you. It needs you to continuously feel secure. As long as you don't have a reason to question yourself, your ego is in no danger of your probing deeper and possibly discovering you have an ego. Therefore, when suddenly you feel insecure about something related to your beliefs, your ego must act quickly. It may send you an impulse to think, *I'm uncomfortable; avoid this.* Or it can make you feel offended. Your ego has a much easier time justifying your opposition by telling you there is something wrong with the new ideas being presented to you, or with the person presenting them, than it would if you were to go digging into the foundations of your beliefs.

As long as any spiritual answers you have leave you no need to disturb your ego, it can exist in its solitude. The concept that God loves you and is waiting for you in the afterlife is one that allows you to be alone while still knowing that God is up there somewhere. The separateness is considered natural—the earthly state of your being. The acceptance of this state is the reconciliation between ego and God. It allows faith in God and the separate being to coexist in you. It allows a religion of separation.

Your ego allows you to accept Jesus Christ as your Savior as long as you also accept you are apart from him; you can be with him after this life if you believe in him. Your ego will let you bask in holy feeling, worship God, and be as religious as you want, as long as you remember your place. You can dance in the sunlight but you are not one with the sun.

As long as you believe that union with God is impossible in this life, your ego is safe in its separation. That is why your ego will so strongly defend Jesus as the only Son of God—the unique and only being who could be one with the Father— something you could never be. Shrouded in piety, the work of ego is hidden from sight. If Jesus was the only Son of God, who are you—the illegitimate child of God?

❦

The ego is a savvy trickster. For example, when you had read the words, "You are already saved," perhaps you were a bit shocked, but you kept on reading. Now imagine a man who read those words and threw the book down in disgust. He might have scoffed and denied the words had any possible value, or he might have gotten angry, believing the words were an assault on his sacred beliefs. Maybe the words seemed so heretical that he thought they came from the devil. At such times, the ego sits back and smiles at a job well done—its position as secure as ever.

Your ego may summon cyclones of anxiety in you rather than leave itself exposed. It may cause you to think that all the discomfort you feel is being caused by the words you are reading. It may tell you that God, Jesus, or the Bible is being attacked. Your ego may tell you that your faith is being attacked. It knows how to strike the deepest chords to rally your defenses.

The ego won't tell you what's really going on: That it's not God, Jesus, the Bible, or your faith being called into question here. *It is the ego that is being called into question.*

You may have been taught you can only be with God after you die, but the truth is, you are with God now, and you could live in conscious union with him. What you cannot do is be separate from God and one with him at the same time. By accepting this truth, you are putting your ego at grave risk— you are telling your ego there is a possibility that a separate being cannot be. And while you may not be consciously aware of what that means, your ego does know—it means its inevitable annihilation. Even if you know that few people, if any, could ever overcome their ego completely, your ego knows only the real threat and does everything in its power to protect itself.

Abandoning the notion that you need to be saved does not mean you are abandoning Jesus Christ. You are only abandoning the belief that you must be separate from God while you are alive. Don't allow the voice of ego (yours or anyone else's) to convince you otherwise.

What all this means is that your ego is not real. It is a construct of your psyche. It seems real and can be difficult to discern because its construction began when you were too young to be aware. However, God and your spirit are real; your ego is not. Your ego is a manifestation of your belief that you are separate from God, or simply separate and alone inside.

Referring to ego as a separate being is a way to help clarify what's going on inside you. Of course you're not crazy and you're not possessed; obviously the ego is a part of you. When we speak about the ego thinking, or as a being, we are talking about you. It's the part of you that thinks of yourself as separate not only from God but also from others, and would have you think that is who you are—your identity as dictated by the world, and your attention kept on that world, rather than turning inward to find who you really are, which the ego does not want.

If you are unaware of how your ego functions, the older you get the more developed it will be, and the harder it will be for you to break free of what you've become accustomed to believing is true. Yet you can never be so old that breaking free is impossible. If you look deep enough inside yourself, you will see that ego is like a great plant growing in a Petri dish—it has no natural roots. You can trace your ego's thoughts down to the true original sin: the incorrect thought of your isolated self, which drives the incorrect ways you can think, speak, and act.

Your ego has only your conscious mind to work with—to hijack and leverage against you so that any momentary insecurity you might feel about facing something unknown quickly grows into full-on fear, which can manifest as anger, disgust, or any number of ways. Yet you know yourself better than your conscious mind is aware. You know that your ego does not define who you are; there is much more to you than that. That is why you are drawn to God. You are predisposed to God, which means you are predisposed to who you truly are—a spiritual being who is at home in God's Spirit and truth, and you will therefore recognize his words.

If you believe in God, you believe that the spirit is eternal; you have a soul. You know the body is the temporary home of that soul. The world is the home of the body. Your ego is as temporal as your life in the world.

Ego the Ally

The ego is not all dismal stuff. As we walk our spiritual path, our ego will rise to challenge us in more ways than can be captured here, by hiding in thoughts too familiar to recognize as ego, and by looking for new ways to tempt us from the truth of our higher self. Once we are aware of how it works, however, we can make a game of catching the little devil at work. We can use ego-driven thoughts as a way to become conscious of what we don't want and clarify what we do want.

For example, someone cuts you off in traffic and you're enraged and give them the finger. Upon reflection, you are bothered that you could let yourself be so easily affected and behave in such a way. You feel badly and don't wish to treat anyone that way. Or maybe you are at a party or a show and find yourself not paying attention to what's being said or happening in front of you, because you're concerned about how you look to others. You then realize that being present is more important to you and are likely to have a better time.

Your ego has been your ally as well as your enemy. The ego is your protector, for better or worse. You may recall from our discussion in chapter 4 that the world of separation begins very early in life—such as on the school playground. Your ego protects itself by making sure you do not stand out, but this also helps you to fit into the world. You act "normal"; you make friends. You develop a sense of safety and security, which can serve you throughout your whole life.

As an adult, you need money to pay for food, shelter, medicine, or anything else you require. Your ego helps you to stay focused on these realities. You are alone, in that God does not physically intervene in this world, so it is important to be self-sufficient. God is with you, but you have to drive the car. You can have the faith of a saint, but take your hands off the wheel and you will crash.

Your ego keeps you grounded. If your experience of God were to become too intense, you might no longer fully respect what is required of reality. You might become delusional—believing that knowing God is enough—and not pay attention to surviving or doing all you must to succeed in the real world. This might work for a dedicated monk but not for anyone who wants to live a balanced life in the ego-dominated world.

If, for example, you were to suppose that since God heals, and you know God, you need not take care of your body. You might then become sick. Your weakened ego would quickly remind you that belief in God, and being realized as one with God (such that no sickness could touch you), are not the same. Or you might be an avid seeker with a great deal of spiritual information, but when someone says something that triggers you to lose your temper, you quickly come to realize how strong your ego is and that you still have work to do if being spiritually realized is your goal. Or perhaps you experience the stark wake-up call of a financial failure. A crushed ego can work wonders to motivate you.

We learn from personal experience. Most of the examples in this section are lessons I learned about my own ego—more often than not, the hard way.

To call the ego the enemy is to discredit the good it does. Your ego is too much a fact of your makeup to not be seen as part of God's plan. Further, to call it the enemy is to empower it against you, because you then view it as something outside your control. You have to accept you have an ego in order to see it, just as the addict must acknowledge the addiction before a new reality can be forged. With this acceptance comes clarity and strength—the knowledge of where you don't want to be and where you do want to go.

⚜

Whether we call it spiritual development, fulfillment, or realization, our desire for a relationship with God has that loftiest of goals—salvation. At some point, we will need to cross the line to allegiance with Spirit; we will have to work toward transcendence of ego. We will have to accept God's promise of a kingdom of Spirit to find. For what is salvation, truly, if not permanent residence in Spirit—union with God?

What if salvation, which you imagine you will experience in heaven, is something you can begin to experience on earth? Fixed on the afterlife in heaven, the road of seeking ends when you are presented with and believe in the Son, and you are told that's as far as you can or need to go. Fixed on God and living your fullest life, the road can begin now with Jesus and his teachings and extend beyond the horizon, as far as you want to go.

CHAPTER 18

SALVATION IS NOW

As with some of the other terms we've discussed, there is a spiritual definition of the word "saved" that is more profound than literally being saved from going to a bad place after we die. The spiritual definition involves our life on earth.

In chapter 9 we discussed John 15:5: "I am the vine, you are the branches. Those who abide in me and I in them bear much fruit, because apart from me you can do nothing." This means we have spiritual life flowing through us so long as we are consciously connected to God, which means we are keeping God and his teachings in our mind and heart and acting accordingly.

To stay connected to God *is* salvation. We can be saved not just because we believe Jesus is divine but because we believe God is real and here for us now, as exemplified by Jesus. By following his example of faith in God, and his teaching us to seek God, we come to know that the divine is in us as well, and we can commune with God within ourselves.

Doesn't the very notion that we should abide in God fundamentally conflict with any teaching that our place is to be separate from God, or to not know him until we get to heaven? If we can't know God now, how could we possibly abide in him? Jesus' words guide us into an active relationship with God. He wants us to know God personally, in our mind, heart, and soul. Salvation is coming to know God now, not in theory for later.

To be saved means to liberate ourselves from fear, from ego-domination, from darkness, from suffering, from limitation, from anything holding us down and preventing us from soaring. Wings are not reserved for angels. Jesus said, "With your faith you can move mountains."[1] Are these mountains not on earth? He said, "Everything is possible for one who believes."[2] Did he mean possible only in heaven? These messages were not the abstract inspirational words of a gracious Messiah; they are part of the truth Jesus lived to let people know. We can live in the same reality of Spirit as Jesus did. But if all we do is look up, imagining divinity is reserved for heaven, we could miss this glorious truth of our lives.

Eternal Life

Eternal life remains the core reward of belief systems founded in Jesus' name. You've been told that eternal salvation will come after this life. But if eternal life is guaranteed for the faithful and it is initiated by your faith now, why do you have to wait for it? Is it because "eternal" refers only

1 Matthew 17:20; Mark 11:23.
2 Mark 9:23.

to the afterlife? Okay, but what happens if your faith wavers before you die? Do you still have eternal life? If it can be taken away, is it truly eternal? Can something be everlasting and at the same time stoppable?

What does the word eternal mean, anyway?

In many dictionaries you will find two definitions of the word "eternal." One is: without beginning or end; the other is: of infinite duration. The one that is the most appropriate depends on the context in which the word is used. When we are talking about the nature of God or Spirit, eternal means without beginning or end, and is usually how Jesus used the word. God is understood as always having been and will always ever be.

When you are told that eternal life will be yours after you die, you know what is meant, but, technically, the idea doesn't make sense. Eternity does not begin at a fixed point in the future and extend forever; it has no beginning. That is why you will not find a single instance in the Bible telling you that eternal life will be yours after you die. The Bible says eternal life will be yours if you believe. It is a critical distinction.

It lends to the understanding that Jesus did not come to show you the way to eternal life later; he came to show you a state that exists now, eternally. It is the kingdom of God. It is the realm of Spirit—always present—like God's forgiveness—eternally true. How his heart yearned for you to see this truth.

Do not be afraid, little flock, for it is your Father's
good pleasure to give you the kingdom.
(Luke 12:32)

Everyone who asks receives.
(Matthew 7:8; Luke 11:10)

Very truly, I tell you, anyone who hears my word
and believes in him who sent me *has* eternal
life, and does not come under judgment, but *has*
passed from death to life.
(John 5:24; emphases added)

In the last verse, if you receive the words of God, and believe in God who is their source, then you have already passed
from spiritual death to eternal life, right here on earth, which
is the main theme of the Gospel of John. You are alive in the
kingdom that has no end and no beginning. That life is everlasting (of infinite duration), unless we slip back into the
mindset of separation (aka sin, not present in faith, not consciously connected to the vine).

That is why Jesus said, "Whoever follows me will never
walk in darkness but will have the light of eternal life."
Follows is a verb—it's not a one-time act but something we
keep doing—practicing faith, and in so doing we walk in the
light, just like *believes* ("in him who sent me") is not the same
as holding one belief, but means constant maintenance. The
light is eternal; the kingdom of Spirit is eternal. Our choice to
consciously live in it, of course, requires diligence, as our

earthly life is full of temptations, distractions, and hardships that we might allow to deter us.

Jesus brought us the gift of knowing that the kingdom is already here for us. What we believe in precedes our belief in it; it existed long before we got here.

This is not to say there is no kingdom called heaven for us to be in after we die, or that life will not be everlasting after death. There has been almost no comment on that thus far; your beliefs are your own. Whatever any of us believes, no one knows for sure what happens to each and every one of us when we die, much less the details of what the place we go to is like, but we *can* know a kingdom on earth. If we do believe that we will still exist after this life, then we must believe there is some heavenly part of us that transcends mortality.

Eternal life is not disconnected from this life. What is our soul but eternal life, housed for a time in our body? We connect with the Spirit of God inside us, within our soul. Ironically, it can be easier to accept a kingdom that exists only in the afterlife because then there is no reason to seek one now. The kingdom is so desired that many of us allow the fate of our souls to depend on our faith in the future kingdom, yet we will ignore the possibility that the kingdom is also available to us right here.

Jesus shows a path that requires discipline and perseverance—the narrow way—to stay righteous and never give up on seeking God, but whose rewards are the entrance into the kingdom of God on earth. Is this too good to be true? We choose the answer according to our faith and seeking. If we are spiritually awake in life, we will be alive in heaven on earth. We don't need to wait until we are dead to walk in the bliss of God and

WHAT THE HELL IS HELL?

know Spirit personally. Or, we can believe this information is not true, and not seek, and thereby give ourselves more proof that there is no kingdom to be found on earth.

Eternal Death

Now let's turn this understanding of what eternal means to the idea of eternal punishment or eternal fire—terms that have scared countless numbers of us, generation upon generation, age after age. We haven't allowed for the possibility of eternal life without eternal death.

Eternal life means no death. In the Gospel of John, Jesus indicates that to believe in him is to not be subject to death:

> For God so loved the world that he gave his one and only Son, that whoever believes in him shall not perish but have eternal life. (John 3:16)

> and everyone who lives and believes in me will never die. (John 11:26)

Death is separation from God, so now we are talking about eternal separation. By not believing in God—not keeping him and his words in mind (which can also be called ignoring wisdom and good sense), we are subject to living only according to our selves and our actions. If we harm ourselves or others (sin), we suffer the result of those actions (death). That harm can also simply be the choice of isolation from God, Spirit, or our best selves.

As we've discussed, this perceived state of separation does not just occur at some point in the future but is also experienced now. The separation, also, is without beginning or end and will always be our fate. Jesus referred to it as "the outer darkness."[1] And if we don't change, our suffering will be continuous. If we refuse to learn lessons, change our ways, or heed God's words, we are fated to not mature in our development in those ways. We repeat our mistakes indefinitely, until we use our lives wisely to learn God's lessons. This self-inflicted punishment is everlasting until we stop the cycle of darkness—until we take part in saving ourselves.

If we believe that God is loving in nature, then surely his system of judgment is also part of a loving process. Wrath is an ancient-school way of thinking. The law of cause and effect is as much a natural part of our existence as the fact that if we roll a ball down a hill, unless it is impeded it won't stop before it reaches the bottom. If we have a fight with someone we love and say something we regret, the judgment we receive (by default) is simply that the other person will be hurt as a result of our actions, and perhaps we'll feel hurt and remorseful as we realize that. Our salvation might be to offer a heartfelt apology. Our condemnation might be some minor, everlasting suffering until we do.

If we cut ourselves, we will bleed. That is the condemnation. Our salvation is learning to be more careful the next time.

The repercussions of our mistakes, weaknesses, sins, faults, and the opportunity they offer to learn and grow are

---

1 Matthew 8:12.

all part of the human experience. We take care of our own judgment just fine, and many of us are quite skilled at punishing ourselves with guilt, pain, and regret—sometimes for years more than anyone else would deem reasonable. But if God is eternal forgiveness and love, our sins in that light often are just us missing the mark. We were already forgiven before the sin. Perhaps seeing ourselves at times as simply acting out of alignment with God in this way would make sin lighter, and make it easier to forgive ourselves and others.

If we can believe God created the world and left us free will, then maybe we were also left a system by which we can either learn from our mistakes or ignore them, thus creating our own outcomes.

Perhaps the closest to anything we might regard as our traditional idea of hell is that the further away we lived from the light in life, is as far from the light as we will be in death. The veil will be lifted; we will be fully revealed in every facet and detail of who we are and all we've done, maybe even feeling the pain or hurt we caused others to experience—what many of us would call the judgment day. Yet perhaps that will not be God's judgment coming from outside of us, but simply be an objective reflection of who we were. Perhaps that reflection could manifest in a myriad of terrifying ways depending on each individual and what they believe terror to be. Who knows. And yet, if we truly believe that God is Love, could Love ever condemn us to exist in permanent separation from the light, with no hope of parole? Could you ever do that to your own child? What is our love to God's Love? Never mind what others say; ask these questions of your own heart.

Consider that condemnation is simply not salvation, and perhaps that is hell enough.

I ask you again, what would it possibly benefit God or you to have you burn in everlasting hellfire? Can we finally be the ones to proclaim this is just plain ridiculous? Or is it still just too irreverent to suggest? We must allow ourselves to break free of this madness.

<hr />

As you've read in earlier chapters, Jesus speaks of no afterlife place called hell in any of the four Gospels. Even if *Gehenna* and its fire are understood to be real, he tells us the only time it could be open for business is on the day of judgment, when he returns to judge all of humanity. There are, however, a couple of places where Jesus does talk about an afterlife heaven.

Where Jesus Speaks of Heaven

In my Father's house there are many dwelling places. If it were not so, would I have told you that I go to prepare a place for you? And if I go and prepare a place for you, I will come again and will take you to myself, so that where I am, there you may be also. And you know the way to the place I am going. (John 14:2–4)

This opening to chapter 14 in John is by far the most important place where Jesus talks about heaven.[1] Yet even here, we will see that while Jesus tells us there is a heaven, he still focuses on our present lives. The verses continue: "Thomas said to him, 'Lord, we do not know where you are going. How can we know the way?' Jesus said to him, 'I am the way, and the truth, and the life. No one comes to the Father except through me.'"[2] But pay attention to what Jesus says next:

> If you know me, you will know my Father also.
> From now on you do know him and have seen him.
> Phillip said to him, 'Lord, show us the Father, and
> we will be satisfied.' Jesus said to him, 'Have I
> been with you all this time, Phillip, and you still do
> not know me? Whoever has seen me has seen the
> Father. How can you say, 'Show us the Father?'
> (John 14:7–9)

What is critical to note here, as has been the recurring central message in the Gospel of John, is that when the disciples believe in Jesus and recognize who he is, they *already have seen* God—they have eternal life in the present. They don't need to wait for heaven; *from now on* they know the Father. Even while

---

1 In chapter 7 we discussed the other place he mentions it, in the Gospel of Luke 23:43. When Jesus is on the cross he says to the man on the cross next to him, "Today you will be with me in Paradise."
2 John 14:5–6.

his disciples' eyes are fixed on heaven and how they will get there, Jesus is telling them that to believe in him and know him now are the same as knowing God now, while they are alive, which will naturally result in a place for them by his side in heaven later. The Gospel shows a two-step process. Step one: believe in Jesus and walk in the light of life now, rather than in the darkness of condemnation; step two: as you now have eternal life, so shall there be a place for you in heaven.

All of us who sometimes have trouble understanding the Gospels should take great solace in the fact that even Jesus' disciples, who lived side by side with him throughout his ministry, were often lost and confused by his teachings (it says so in the Gospels, anyway). Fortunately, we have the opportunity to sit with and study his words until the messages become clear. Many of us are so focused on going to heaven that, just as the disciples did, we slight the potential for our lives on earth by not appreciating enough that God is here for us to know right now.

Jesus teaches spirituality based on life, not death. He tells us to love and seek God now. He teaches us how to perceive the kingdom now. He tells us to be a good person now and to love everyone. He tells us to renounce sin—to stop choosing to be separate from God. No matter what we want to believe happens after we die, or at the end of the world, Jesus wants us to be fulfilled and to know God now.

He is God not of the dead, but of the living.
(Matthew 22:32; Mark 12:27; Luke 20:38)

Strive first for the kingdom of God and his
righteousness ... do not worry about tomorrow,
for tomorrow will bring worries of its own.
Today's trouble is enough for today.
(Matthew 6:33–34)

He tells us plainly here not to worry about tomorrow. Doesn't that seem to contradict the notion that we should be not simply worried but downright terrified of not making it into heaven when we die? He tells us to strive for the kingdom of God and righteousness in the same sentence. We could not strive for righteousness if it were not an earthly matter and it is the same for the kingdom of God in this context. And why would Jesus say to strive for the kingdom at all if we only needed to believe in him? It is in times like this—when confusion and contradictions arise—that we might be told something like, "God's ways are not our own. He is beyond our understanding." God is beyond our understanding, but the words in the Bible are there for no purpose other than our understanding.

Jesus' most important evangelist, Paul, beseeches us in his letters to find the rewards of Spirit, which he says are here for us now.

To set the mind on the flesh is death, but to set the
mind on Spirit is life and peace. (Romans 8:6)

God's love has been poured into our hearts
through the Holy Spirit that has been given to us.
(Romans 5:5)

The second verse says that God's love and Holy Spirit
have already been given to us. Do these messages lead you
to keep your attention on the rewards of death? Do they
sound like they are in any way intended to evoke fear? The
time of your salvation is now. Don't worry about eternity;
eternity will bring worries of its own. Today's trouble is
enough for today.

Now is the time to move away from the fearful ancient
belief that the only meaning for your life is to learn what you
need for salvation after death. Now is the time to free yourself from the fear that ignores Jesus' full range and depth of
spiritual teachings in favor of a single ultimatum: choose
heaven or hell. Now is the time to free yourself to seek and find
the kingdom that Jesus lived, labored, suffered, and died to
present to you. To know the kingdom of Spirit is to know you
are part of it. Don't reconcile yourself to remaining a separate
being in a separate world—a purgatory on earth—until death
brings your salvation. Choose the spiritual life that Jesus offered you now.

Free yourself from ultimatums. Find the love first; learn
what's right second. Jesus would rather you be happy than

have the right answers. Jesus would rather you feel the love inside you than even know his name. Free yourself from any fear entwined in what you believe, by remembering to equate God with love, through and through.

CHAPTER 19

LIBERATION

John Restored

I am the way, and the truth, and the life. No
one comes to the Father except through me.
(John 14:6)

Whoever believes in him is not condemned, but
whoever does not believe stands condemned
already because he has not believed in the name
of God's one and only Son. (John 3:18)

Remember that in both these situations Jesus is talking as
the fully realized Son of God. He is the Christ. This is Christ
talking directly to you. A good way to see this is to remove the
name Jesus from your thoughts for a moment. Think of the
Son of God here as pure Spirit, as God on earth. Spirit stands

in a body before you and says, "I am the way, and the truth, and the life. No one comes to the Father except through me." Spirit stands before you and says, "Whoever believes in me is not condemned, but whoever does not believe is condemned already, because he has not believed in the Spirit on earth."

God stands before you and says, "Those who abide in me and I in them bear much fruit, because apart from me you can do nothing."

For so long, many of us have developed an idea of who Jesus Christ is based solely on the biblical stories about him, as seen from the perspective of our own life experience. We all relate to what we know, so we understand the "human" him as we know ourselves, leaving the unknown "godly" him as beyond our understanding. In other words, we understand his divinity in human terms; we understand divinity itself as something other than us and eternally beyond us. As a result, a personality has been imprinted onto the name Jesus—the Lord, the Savior, the one and only Son of God—who is separate and removed from us...from you.

If only there were a way to understand and use those titles spiritually, rather than in human terms of absolute exclusivity that perpetuate the separation.

If you accepted the reconciliation of ego and God: Jesus is up there and you are down here; he is the Savior and you a lowly sinner. The relationship is exactly as it should be, according to a belief system of separation. You may feel his presence and guidance in your life, but he is fundamentally different from you. Jesus is the Son of God, after all, and you know you are not.

How Jesus labored and beckoned your soul to see who

you truly are—how like him you are—beloved by God, with open-ended possibility for your relationship with God. In better recognition of who you are, you could be ever-inspired in your seeking to know God better. Jesus knew that the kingdom of God is in you. Jesus knew what people were not ready to hear:

Only through yourself can you know God.

Only through yourself can you know anything. Remember what we discussed back in chapter 1 about learning to drive? You can't learn to drive by sitting in a classroom; you have to get behind the wheel and practice. Only through yourself—through your own experience of making mistakes and correcting them—do you become better. Or, remember the difference between memorizing multiplication tables and understanding the principle of multiplication? Two sticks two times gives you four sticks.

Or consider someone with whom you fell deeply in love. Chances are, you did not feel that way the moment you met, unless it was love at first sight. Either way, true, lasting love grows from intimate interaction and experience.

All this is also true about your relationship with God. You can believe in God with all your heart. You can love God with everything you are. But you can grow in your understanding of God only through your own experience of him. If you don't already, would you like to know God now, rather than just believe in or pray to him?

Would you like to know for yourself which are the words of God and which are the words of people? Come to know spiritual truth through yourself and you will become an authority on the Bible.

Trust yourself to determine what is truth. Trusting only in an outside source is for those who have not trusted in their own capacity to understand the words of God. For spiritual matters, stay true to the source that defines you: your relationship with God. Walking your own path is the only way you can know anything. Come to know, rather than settle for belief.

If you keep on seeking, one day you are going to find that, as you learn who you are, you will learn for yourself who Jesus Christ was/is. You will come to understand him and relate to him through your own spiritual knowledge, gained through your own spiritual experience. These are not religious words. Your knowledge of Jesus, or God, will always be a perfect reflection of what you know of yourself. This is because:

There is no separation.

The only separation possible is the one you choose to imagine and believe in—you can stay fixed on the idea of it. God is here with you now. The kingdom is not a place you find, or get to; it is where you already live. If you stay true to the path of seeking and never give up on its course, you will arrive at the truth:

You are one with God.

Call it God, Christ, Allah, Spirit, Yahweh, or any of the other names given to a higher power since the dawn of humanity, we're made from the same stuff. You may believe

you can only be one with God when you die. You may believe only Jesus could be one with the Father while he was
alive. You may believe that if you follow the path of seeking
long enough, you could one day attain oneness with God. The
truth is, you are one with God right now. You just may not be
aware of it. You may not believe it, but you cannot be separate
from God.

"No one comes to the Father except through me."

"Me" is you.

"Whoever believes in the only Son of God is not
condemned."

You are the Son of God.

Does this sound blasphemous to you—to call yourself the
Son of God?

It is written that when Jesus was at a feast in Jerusalem,
a mob surrounded him, saying, "If you are the Messiah, tell
us plainly," to which Jesus replied, "The Father and I are
one." The mob picked up stones to stone him, accusing him
of blasphemy that a mere man should claim to be God. Jesus
answered, "Is it not written in your law, 'I said, you are gods'?
If those to whom the word of God came were called 'gods,'
can you say that the one whom the Father has sanctified

and sent into the world is blaspheming because I said I am God's Son?"[1]

Jesus is referring to Psalm 82, in which God addresses a heavenly assembly he calls "gods" (those to whom the word of God came), who were tasked with governing the nations. Jesus is basically saying to his accusers: If in your own law[2] anyone other than God can be called gods, why shouldn't I be able to call myself that?

The tricky thing about spiritual words is that you interpret them according to your own spiritual understanding. When Jesus said, "I and the Father are one," he spoke his own truth. To others his truth seemed like blasphemy.

He spoke this truth, according to what's written, because Jesus Christ on earth was the fully realized spiritual being— the fully realized Son of God, unconstrained by ego. He was the expression of oneness with God; God in the flesh. There was no bushel basket over his flame; the light shone purely, like the sun.

The light preached to you that you too could shine like this. You have the same light inside you, and Jesus wanted to bring it out of you—to set it on a hill for all to see—as if to say, *Behold, I am; as I am, so too can you be.*[3] The good news was for you. That you believe in Jesus as your Lord—that he was sanctified and sent into the world by God—should cause you to accept his message concerning your own capability and his wish for your realization—to follow him down that road. He

---

1 John 10:22–36.

2 The Jewish scriptures.

3 "You are the light of the world. A city built on a hill cannot be hid" (Matthew 5:14).

spoke as you, for you, to show you who you are. To consider him fundamentally different from you is to deny this part of his message for you.

The Son of God[4] is the spirit within you. It is your soul. It is your true identity. The Son of God is Christ within you. Your spiritual path is one of accepting your true, higher self —your Self. There is only one Son living through all of us, of which you are a part, and which is a part of God. Whoever sees the Son of God within themselves sees who Jesus was and who Christ is. These are not religious words.

⊷⊱⊰⊱⊰⊱⊰⊱⊰

It might seem that to accept yourself as the Son of God is the worst blasphemy you could ever conceive because it sounds like you're claiming to be equal to Jesus Christ. Remember, however, that to acknowledge the divinity in yourself is not the same as declaring yourself to be a fully realized spiritual being. You are declaring that you are a spiritual being with the *potential* to be fully realized. By doing this, you are accepting one of the Gospels' main lessons.

It would indeed be blasphemous to state that you are the fully realized Christ in the flesh when you are not. Yet it would be equally blasphemous to state that you never could be.

The distinction between you and Jesus is one of realized potential. When you understand that, you turn the wall that separated you from God into an open door. It is the "open

---

4 Or the Daughter of God—same meaning. The Son is not a term of gender here but a term of universal spirit.

door, which no one is able to shut."[1] Even though Jesus promised us we could find the kingdom of God and know God, people's egos denied it almost immediately after Jesus said the words. That denial was like another fall from grace.

Your ego does not want you to accept your divinity. Your ego wants you to accept your separation from Jesus Christ, who was unique among all human beings who ever lived or ever will live. Comfort in separation is the game of the ego. But you know better now. You are quickened with the words your soul can recognize.

As the fully realized living God, Jesus was love incarnate. As he lived, he could not help loving you and all his fellow human beings. Jesus acted as the great pioneer who found the Promised Land downriver and shouted back for you to follow. He did not intend for you to know the Promised Land only after you died. He led you to the truth that God has been with you all along, even though you may not have been consciously aware of it.

It would be correct for *you* to say, "No one can come to the Father, except through me"—"me" being the spirit within you. The only Spirit you can know is the one you are a part of (not apart from). Jesus' saying these words with reference to himself means they are true for you as well, because he spoke as Spirit, as Christ, and Christ is within you.

On that day you will know that I am in my Father, and you in me, and I in you. (John 14:20)

---

1 Revelation 3:8.

Your soul is in your body. God is found within you. Like most of us, you may not yet have spent enough time learning about Spirit to fully understand the implications of the words "except through me" to the depth Jesus did, but the same truth is waiting for you. The truth is always the truth. Many roads of seeking lead to this one master truth:

You are god.

This is another way to identify who you truly are—your Self; "god" is another way of saying Son of God. The life of Spirit on earth that dwells within each one of us is god; it is an identity we all have in common. You can cling to the delusion that you are separate as long as you choose; you can be a slave to your ego your entire life. Or, you can set yourself free by acknowledging the truth of your godly nature.

A few pages ago you saw Psalm 82:6 cited, which Jesus quoted to those accusing him of blasphemy for referring to himself as God's Son. In the full verse, God says to his heavenly assembly, "You are gods, children of the Most High, all of you." If you believe that Jesus chose his words carefully and with purpose, then he did so when he cited this verse and used this vocabulary for us to relate to.

If God can refer to any others beside himself as "gods," and if you believe God created you and blessed you by sending you into this world, should it be blasphemy for you to consider yourself the Son or Daughter of God? Perhaps God wants us living in that knowledge, just as long as we stay humble to the truth of our current place—how fully we are living in that identity and how much of our potential is fulfilled.

Look to the words of both Jesus and Paul, as they applied this language to you. Jesus said, "Love your enemies, do good ... and you will be children of the Most High."[1] This is whom Jesus beseeched you to become. It is part of the good news being delivered to you. Paul wrote, "For all who are led by the Spirit of God are children of God."[2] Who does that leave out?

Christ is the living God; it is god within you. Christ is not only within you, Christ is you. And Christ in all of us together is the kingdom. These are not my words; they are Christ's words. And strange as it may seem, these are not religious words. They are words of spiritual meaning. Union is the truth, and separation has been the delusion.

⋆⁂⋆⁂⋆

You are a magnificent child of God for whom anything is possible. Now you can more intimately understand the words, "No one knows the Father except the Son," and likewise, "no one knows the Son, except the Father"—only you can know God through yourself and no one knows you like God. If you relentlessly seek God, you will come to know him intimately, and you will know him more each day, which is to know yourself more as well.

Once you overcome all your fears, relinquish all ideas of separation, embody love as a fully realized shining beacon of

---

1 Luke 6:35; Matthew 5:44–45 similarly says, "Love your enemies and pray for those who persecute you, so that you may be children of your Father in heaven."
2 Romans 8:14.

300

light in the world, and you live in perpetual, conscious union with God because he is living fully in the flesh through you, then you can say that you are [state your name] Christ.

Maybe you will not get there, but God's truth says you can.

The tables have turned. A new mob in Christ's name might say, "Who are you, a mere person, to call yourself the Son of God?" In love you can answer, "I am who the Lord tells me I am." Or fear can prompt you to recoil from and reject everything you've been reading here.

It may seem humble to limit yourself to just worshiping the Son of God. But, in truth, you are then not living up to the ideal that Jesus said was possible for you. And so, in fact, you are saying you know better than Jesus. You are saying you know better than God. You are saying, "I am *not* the light of the world." "I am *not* a child of God."

You don't want to be governed by your ego any longer, do you?

A lifetime of beliefs and practices—a way of thinking—does not come undone in a day, nor is it meant to. If you want to take a few seeking steps in a new direction, you will move at the speed that is best for you, and you will regularly find yourself in just the right place on your path.

None of us is perfect. Even Jesus Christ—the Son who walked in fully realized divinity—had moments of doubt. Hours before his arrest, which he knew would lead to his crucifixion, he prayed: "My Father, if it is possible, let this cup pass from me."[1] And when he was on the cross, he cried out: "My God, my God, why have you forsaken me?"[2]

These words show the humanity of Jesus. They should bond you to him, and to the truth of your godliness even in your imperfection. Jesus did not intend for you to consider him different in nature from yourself. That he was the same as you (in being, soul, and living potential) is the salvation he presents you—it is your bridge to the kingdom of God.

Free your mind, heart, and soul. You are the living god. You can rest in humility and love, knowing that everyone else is god too. The only difference in this regard between one person and another is the degree to which each one has accepted who they are and realized their spirit in the world.

You are the way, the truth, and the life. Can you believe this? Will you listen to Jesus? He said:

> nor will they say, "Look, here it is!" or "There it is!" For, in fact, the kingdom of God is within you. (Luke 17:21)

Hear the Gospel with your own ears. Read it with your own eyes. Recognize it through your own soul. Don't look outside yourself. Don't look anywhere else. The kingdom of God is found only within you.

---

1 Matthew 26:39; Mark 14:36; Luke 22:42. "Let this cup pass from me" is a metaphor—he doesn't want to drink the fate of suffering that is in the cup.
2 Mark 15:34; Matthew 27:46.

Realize the god within you. Fighting your union with God is like a drop of water trying to separate itself from the rest of the ocean. But that is what most of us spend a lifetime doing.

Save yourself from ignoring the fullest extent of the love God has for you and what God wants you to know. You will be saved from your own fear. You will be saved from your ego. If your life tends to be a living hell, you will be saved from hell.

You will rejoice in love. You will dance in happiness. You will glow in spiritual realization. You will speak the word of God. You will live as your Self. You will know heaven on earth.

CHAPTER 20

EXALTATION

Do not fear fear anymore.

Joy joy!

The kingdom of God is at hand. It was in your midst all along.

You are the light of the world. Let your light shine in the world.

You are the doorway through which love enters the world.

Dance and sing and leap for joy! For fear is no more. Fear has always been a choice. Fear has always been ignor-ance. Fear has always been ignoring what Christ tells you—not told you, for the word is living in the present.

The words above are pure in meaning. Do not allow them to be hijacked by religious interpretation.

Take fear out of the word Christ.

Christ is just a word of spiritual understanding, which re-fers to the Son of God.

Disempower religious words. Do not give them
control over you.

Words are just words. They have no spiritual meaning
beyond what you give them.

Take the stigma out of the word God.

If you can't take fear out of the word God just yet, try
replacing it with the word Love for a while and see how your
experience changes.

Disempower your religion; do not give it
control over you.

Religion is just religion. It is not God. Religion is here to
serve you; you are not here to serve religion.

If your religion serves your well-being it is a blessing.
Religion's beautiful function is guiding your relationship with
God, teaching you about love, Spirit, seeking, and joining you
with other like-minded believers. Religion can also be a good
way to keep you part of a community.

If you are troubled by aspects of your religion, however,
or find contradictions between what you feel about God and
what you are being taught, take a break. Your religion won't
go anywhere. Don't be afraid to do what's right for you—that's
what's important. If you are afraid, it's a sign that something
is wrong. You are love incarnate; that's why fear feels wrong.
Nurturing the love within you is what matters most. Whatever

church, place of worship, belief system, or practice you choose as a means to serve your relationship with God, make sure the choice comes purely from you and not from fear of disagreeing with or diverging from a choice that was made for you by others.

Disempower the Bible. Do not give it control over you.

The Bible is just a book—perhaps the greatest book ever written; perhaps not. The Bible is not the Gospel, though the Gospel resides there. The human ego let in some bad news too—as a long-term tenant. The Bible is here to serve you; you are not here to serve the Bible.

You are the Son or Daughter of God, and so is everyone else. Be-loved, manifest more fully who you are.

<hr>

Free yourself from the notion that there is only one way to find God or spiritual understanding.

There are many ways and places to learn in the world. There are books that will change the way you see everything, written thousands of years ago, hundreds of years ago, decades ago, last week. Open yourself up to learn from spiritual sources other than the Bible. Other perspectives can often help you to understand the same universal truths. Hindu spiritual texts might shed light on a sentence of Gospel that you never quite understood. Buddhism teaches you to free yourself from the suffering that results from a continuous cycle of darkness and ignorance, which is exactly what Jesus taught.[1] Literature from Native Americans might guide you to a deeper connection to the earth. Only the fear generated and used against you by your ego would deny you access to the whole of God's great library.

> Free yourself from what others tell you are the words of God or who they tell you God is.

Though many good teachers will teach you, do not take at face value any truth told to you. As we discussed in chapter 1, blind faith can be like a beautiful flower cut from its roots, which of itself will grow you little, versus the practicing faith of your personal seeking, which is the whole flower growing from its roots. Believe only what you find through your own seeking to be true.

> Practice freeing yourself from fear until you do.

Fear has never been anything but the servant of separation. To choose fear is to make a conscious choice to believe you are separate from God. It is to believe a lie. You cannot choose fear and love at the same time. To free yourself from fear, you

---

1 "If your eye is unhealthy, your whole body will be full of darkness. If then the light in you is darkness, how great is the darkness!" (Matthew 6:23)

don't need to fight fear. Choose love, and fear will evaporate. The great news is that love is the truth of who God is and who you are. To choose love is to choose the truth over a lie.

God is Love. You are god. You are love itself.

The only hope of knowing God is to know yourself. Humbly submit to what you know and don't know at this time, even if it means you don't understand some of the things Jesus said, or don't fully understand who he was, or have doubts about any of the stories you've been told, or if you have any questions at all. As you seek them, the answers will come.

To understand Spirit is to know that you grow in Spirit constantly. Depending on your passion for seeking, you can grow one spiritual day over the course of a whole life, or you can grow a whole spiritual life every day. Who you were yesterday is not who you will be today, and you will be new again tomorrow.

In chapter 1 we discussed the tree whose trunk stays true to its roots but whose branches extend and re-leaf each season. Being reborn is not a one-time thing. It happens many times over the course of your spiritual life. It can happen every day. You simply need to be open to letting Spirit show you who you are now, and be ever open and ready to allow the new lessons to come. There is more to find on earth than you dream of there being in heaven. If you have faith not just in God but in the truth that you can know God now, you will come to know

God now. This is not some fluffy inspirational talk. This is the plain truth. These are facts.

> I have told you I am within you. I have told you to seek me for yourself. Jesus told you this. Faith in God and faith in yourself are one and the same. I made you to find me; believe it. Don't display your great faith by believing in me. Prove your faith by finding me.
>
> If you have this faith, you will find me, and you will know me. If you do not have this faith, you will not know me, and you will only be able to believe in me and make what other assumptions you will. A separate being thinks in separate ways.
>
> I am you; you are me; know that we are one. The time is now. I am at hand. This is the Good News.

> Free the name Jesus from religion.

This does not mean removing Jesus from religion. This does not say a religion created in Jesus' name can't serve us well. It means Jesus and religion should not be inextricably linked. Jesus created no religion. Religions were built in his name after his death. It is important not to lose sight of this reality so that the man-made institutions do not become labeled as God-made, and religious principles do not become labeled as God's principles. These religions serve Jesus' purposes—for us to internalize his messages and help us on our path of salvation. But we do not need religion to act as a chaperone between us and him. Our personal relationship with God is our own; religion is simply there to guide and assist that relationship if we so choose.

God is sacred. The religions created in his name are not.

This is not a call to abandon religion. This is not a denunciation of religion. It is a reminder that religion is not supposed to have power over us. Religion is there to serve our relationship with God, which it can do remarkably well, and that warrants reverence. But our love, happiness, and spiritual development were never meant to be bounded within religious doctrine. Our personal connection with God is paramount, and it requires no outside help to facilitate, and knows no bounds.

Would you agree that a religion in Jesus' name is ideally an organization of people who share the same beliefs and gather together in love and in the presence of God to share and explain his messages and to learn and grow together? Then it follows that the gathering should be without fear, sanctimony, dreary services, ultimatums, threats, judgment or condemnation of others, or the belief that there's nothing more to learn. The love of God should be as pure as the laughter of a three-year-old being tickled.

Over the course of the last few decades, at least within my scope, there has been a noticeable shift in the amount of churches and ministries whose members gather together to serve God, love, and community without serving the fear agenda. Perhaps you have noticed too. Love does seem to progress naturally as we serve our spiritual natures. But, as much as we foster the love, it doesn't serve us to bury the fear. There is still an overwhelming amount of fear out there—damnation, hellfire, and a refusal to evolve in our belief systems connected to Jesus. Can we believe in God's love without presuming we need fear to keep us in faith?

Would Jesus want you to be worried or fearful about how to understand him? Or would he rather you be happy and loving God? Would he rather you seek for yourself or only be told the answers? Would he rather you love all your fellow human beings and not believe in him, or worship him daily and not love all your fellow human beings? Your heart knows the answers.

Believing in a future kingdom of heaven you'll go to after you die has its place and is your choice, but this belief should not be at the expense of the kingdom of Spirit present for you to know now. If you are still unsure of this eternal present that you can know now, I believe that if you now keep on reading the Gospels for yourself, all the way through each one, you will find that teaching you how to find and enter the kingdom is one of Jesus' most prominent and repeated messages.

And if you can wake up while you're alive to the perspective of heaven on earth, and you can appreciate the grand wonder and beauty of this life—how special this whole existence is—you will shed tears of shivering awe and joy. You will be filled with a love that is overwhelming beyond words and expression. You will love who you are and you will know that loving every person is the only way to be in perfect harmony with God.

If you suffer, or live in spiritual bondage, I hope you will break free and break through. All the power is within you. By whatever name you call it, the great Spirit is with you, guiding you, blessing you, and loving you. You are the joy of the world.

Stop and smell a lily each day.

Afterword

The Gospels are four dense books, yet perhaps we can summarize the messages of Jesus in terms of his two highest commandments: love God and love others. If each of us did no more than love others in our hearts and in practice, we would have peace on earth. The messages of Jesus were simple. Our egos made them complicated. This book has focused mostly on his first commandment: Love God.

To love God is to seek God. When we are in a relationship with a person we love, if we did nothing more than worship that person, the relationship would not last. We need to work at it with determination and commitment in order to make the relationship work. The same holds true for our relationship with God. We declare our love for God by seeking him/she/it daily, which is also to stay aware and attuned to our higher selves. But that doesn't have to be a rigorous, ascetic struggle. It can simply mean having a desire, an intention, and setting some time aside for the seeking.

For all the great value of congregation with others, we

must also put in the time to be alone with God. That might mean reading, meditating, strolling in a park and letting our thoughts unwind, or just sitting up in bed at night. But we have to make the time. Why? Because the rewards are worth it. Being consciously in tune with God—actually perceiving that God is with us, hearing his guidance, thinking higher thoughts, speaking and acting in a wiser manner, living a life governed by love—sounds enticing, doesn't it?

Having accepted Jesus' instruction to seek, how exactly do we do that? It seems only sensible that we first have to believe in a God or Spirit present here and now. The surest way then to seek God or Spirit is through meditation. I say this based on my own experience, as well as the advice of every spiritual teacher I respect and have learned from. I believe it is what Jesus referred to when he said, "When you pray, go into your room, close the door and pray to your Father, who is unseen."[1]

The privacy of our own consciousness is where we commune with God. While I've certainly had plenty of revelations take place outdoors or in public—sometimes at the least expected times or in the least expected places—meditation is practiced in a controlled, ideally quiet environment, with no distractions, where we can travel deeper and deeper within ourselves.

"Meditate" (in order to know God, or to find peace and clarity) is something you may have heard preached and prescribed so many times throughout your life that it sounds like a cliché. But sometimes clichés are the simple result of the truth always being the truth. This is one truth repeated by

1 Matthew 6:6.

prophets and sages since time immemorial that you don't want to ignore.[2]

Many of us don't try to meditate because it sounds too intimidating. Instead of setting unrealistic goals such as, "Starting tomorrow I'm going to meditate every morning and night for an hour," say that you will commit to meditating every day for some length of time, even if it is no more than five to ten minutes. You can gradually increase the amount of time—even if it's just by one minute each week. It's not necessary to keep track of time, but it can be helpful in the beginning as you get used to the process. There are no rules about how much time you should spend at each sitting, but making the time daily is key.

Meditating can be difficult at first if you're not used to quieting your mind, but you get used to it fairly soon and the rewards come quickly. It's a pretty simple process: have on loose-fitting clothes (if possible; not required), sit comfortably on the floor or in a chair with your back and neck straight, close your eyes, and just be—open and receptive. You want to practice the art of not thinking; as rambling thoughts may come, let them go. Focusing on your breath, in and out, can help with that.

Sometimes I like to start by saying, "Please tell me anything I should hear today," or I just intend to let go and connect with more than myself. You might start by saying a prayer to God, or Jesus, or some other spiritual figure you believe in, or perhaps you have another understanding of God, and then

---

2 If you want more instruction in meditation, you can easily find abundant material on the subject in books, on audio, online, or now there are even a plethora of cell phone apps to help guide you.

WHAT THE HELL IS HELL?

sit receptively and with patience. One need not say a word, or even believe in a higher power, and can just sit and allow clarity or wisdom to come. If you can only sit there for five to ten minutes in the morning, at least you will have the experience of sitting still each day. Even that short amount of time can alter the trajectory of your day for the better, and the days can change your life.

Perhaps you will gain some insight into a problem you were having. Or maybe you will simply feel refreshed, or more alive. Sooner than later you may find yourself wanting to spend more time in that state. One day you will have your moment of connecting with something greater than yourself. Once you experience yourself knowing more—perceiving God more—and evolving as a spiritual being, you might get hooked. Meditation helps every area in your life because it helps you, which in turn helps everything you do.

In cooperation with seeking inward is seeking outward, such as studying the Bible, its history, and what theologians or scholars have to say about the interpretation of its words. You can seek and find renowned books on schools of spirituality with which you are unfamiliar, or listen to lectures or debates on spiritual topics in person or online. By always seeking new sources you move into the unknown. You feed that wonderful gift of a mind you've been given, and as your mind digests what it's been fed, you evolve in your thinking. If you don't agree with something you chose to read or hear, it serves you in knowing why you don't like it. However you choose to do it, remember the ultimate reward you're promised for seeking: nothing less than finding God.

I have found that the requisite complement to seeking is having love be our fundamental disposition and intention. We cannot get far in our seeking without it. This is the perfection of God's system. Seeking without love will find something, because all seeking does, but it will miss the full meaning—the feeling—the deepest fulfillment of who we are as beings of love.

When we give in to love, any ordinary moment can blossom into something extraordinary, and us with it. We can consciously raise our awareness in whatever we are doing. We can think and feel with love and work it into any moment—into a conversation we are having with anyone (by paying complete attention to and appreciating them), into our meditations and thoughts about God or Spirit (feeling our desire to have God flood through us and guide us), into the experience of the nature around us (breathing in the air; seeing, hearing, and appreciating our surroundings)—you name it. As we choose love, our perceptions and feelings expand exponentially, the way a gray day transforms when the sun emerges from the passing clouds.

Have you ever had the experience of being home and you put on one of your favorite songs, crank it up, and it's playing in the background while you do some other stuff, but your love of the song overtakes you, you break out in a big smile and start dancing freely in the purest of fun? The music expands to greater dimension—somehow becoming more of itself—while you become more of yourSelf. You become one with the music and your joy expands like sunshine in your living room. The song ends, and you stand there vibrating in a whole other place of being than you were five minutes ago.

Well, the experience is available, anyway.

The amazing thing is, when we bring that feeling into our seeking, into our processing of God's words, without the fear of eternal stakes, that same joy runs through us and tells us everything we need to know. Spirit speaks through feeling as much as through thought. An organ and some gospel singers might convey God's love better than any of our words can.

We can learn a great deal of spiritual knowledge with just our mind, but love is the key to the kingdom of Spirit. We can try to deny this. We can also try to jump high enough to defy gravity. We are beings of love, and learning to live according to this truth is to be at peace and in harmony with who we are. We can just be still and know love is.

⚜

Jesus wanted you to know God—not just as some far off, incomprehensible supreme being to whom you pray, but as one with whom you can actually communicate. If you seek God, God will make Godself known to you in ways that only you will know. Spirit will show you that something more is going on than mere blatant reality. You'll receive custom-tailored communications. Perhaps you will receive what seems like an intuition of spiritual understanding; maybe there will be some kind of wink of uncanny coincidence; or maybe you'll find yourself hearing just the right words at the right time. You will be amazed. *How is it possible that there are more than seven billion people on this planet and yet God has heard and spoken to me? How can God be guiding me and also all those other people?*

While we may not comprehend how this happens, it is nonetheless true and can be experienced by anyone who chooses to seek God, and never gives up. Faith that God exists is a good starting point, but faith that you can know God, followed by intention and the action of seeking, is a faith to which God responds.

The path begins with this kind of faith.

I am not a Bible scholar or a preacher, but I take writing about the Bible as seriously as one can. I spent thousands of hours on this project over several years, researching the Bible and crafting the words just right. However, that does not make me an expert or a perfect writer, and this text will always be open to revision when it is warranted. If you found anything incorrect in this book—with content or even a typo—or you have comments, suggestions, would like to join discussion groups, or work one-on-one with me, you can visit:

whatishell.com

or

kevingrantauthor.com

If you valued or enjoyed this book, *please* take a moment to post a review where you bought it. It helps so much in attracting others to read it. Thank you!

Printed in Great Britain
by Amazon